Ngũgĩ wa Thiong'o (1938–2025) was a Kenyan novelist, playwright, and critic whose work chronicles colonialism, dictatorship, and resistance, and who championed writing in Gĩkũyũ and translation among African languages. Imprisoned in 1977 and later exiled, he taught at several US universities, including UC Irvine.

I0876302

THE AFRICA LIST

NGŨGĨ WA THIONG'O

The Language of Languages

REFLECTIONS ON TRANSLATION

Seagull Books
LONDON NEW YORK CALCUTTA

Seagull Books, 2026

First published in volume form by Seagull Books, 2023

This volume is not for sale in East Africa (Kenya, Tanzania and Uganda)

ISBN 978 1 80309 696 4

British Library Cataloguing-in-Publication Data
A catalogue record for this book is available from the British Library

Typeset at Seagull Books, Calcutta, India

Contents

Editorial Note

This volume brings together lectures and talks given by Ngũgĩ wa Thiong'o at different venues between 2000 and 2019. Ideas and anecdotes recur through these essays. We have chosen to retain these repetitions so that this volume may function as an accurate record of the author's substantial contributions in the field of translation.

Translation

Towards a Global Conversation among Languages and Cultures

I am glad to be here, my very first time, in the land of Gabriela Mistral, Nicanor Parra, Pablo Neruda, Victor Jara, Isabel Allende, and Ariel Dorfman. So many literary greats from Chile! I never of course met Gabriel Mistral, Nicanor Parra, Victor Jara, nor have I met Isabel Allende; but I have had the honour of interacting with Ariel Dorfman and once, in 1966, with Pablo Neruda.

I met Ariel Dorfman during his professorship at Duke University; but more importantly, when in the late 90s, a group of us founded the first Gĩkũyũ-language journal, *Mũtiiri*, he allowed us to carry translations of his poem 'Last Will and Testament / Testamento'.[1] It was the first-ever translation of a Chilean poet into an African Language, and our new journal, then

Keynote at the Global Humanities Institute 2019: Challenges of Translation, Santiago, Chile, 25 July 2019.

1 Ariel Dorfman, 'Last Will and Testament / Testamento' in *In Case of Fire in a Foreign Land: New and Collected Poems from Two Languages* (Edith Grossman trans.) (Durham, NC: Duke University Press, 2002).

in print but now online, was privileged to carry the translations done by a Kenyan, Professor Gĩtahi Gĩtiti, directly from its Spanish original under the title 'Marũa ma Kwĩgaya'.

My first and last face-to-face encounter with Pablo Neruda was much earlier, in New York, at the 1966 PEN International Conference, which for the first time brought together writers from the communist East, the Western capitalist bloc, and those from Asia, Africa and South America under the general theme: The Writer as an Independent Spirit. The American writer Arthur Miller, president of PEN International at the time, had worked hard to ensure the waiver of visas for those previously barred from the USA on account of their communist affiliations. It was a conference that tried to bridge the Cold War divide.

I was then a postgraduate student at Leeds University, but it was as an author of two novels—*Weep Not, Child* (1964) and *The River Between* (1965)—that I got the invitation, with the added designation of regional guest of Africa, to parallel other regional guests of honour representing other continents. I was both thrilled and awed by the occasion, and mostly I sat back to absorb and enjoy the literary atmosphere.

And then came a panel, one of the last, which included Ignazio Silone, the Italian author of *Bread and Wine* (1936), and Pablo Neruda, with Arthur Miller as the chair. I was still half lost in my enjoyment of the atmosphere when I heard Silone complain about the lack of translations of modern Italian writing into English, adding: '[. . .] And you know, Italian is not like one of these Bantu languages with one or two words in their vocabulary.'

Gone was my enjoyment of the literary atmosphere. The honour of a continent was under attack. I stood up to object to the insult to Africa. After all, I was the regional guest of honour, assuring the audience that African languages were equal to any other, and certainly had more than two words in their vocabulary.

Later, at a crowded reception, Pablo Neruda walked across to me and shook my hand. My Spanish was zero and he was hesitant in his English, but I have always appreciated that gesture, coming soon after that confrontation over Silone's characterization of African languages. More than the literary atmosphere, it was this encounter with Neruda that left a lasting impression on me. I took this as a gesture of solidarity with my anguished but defiant rejoinder on the language question.

Later, my rejoinder came to haunt me when I returned to Leeds and resumed my work on my third novel: *A Grain of Wheat* (1967). I was writing it in English. But had I not just come from New York where I talked about the wealth of African languages? This question would set in motion a series of thoughts and doubts and actions, which, years later, would lead me into a maximum-security prison, and then, into abandoning English as the primary language of my creative imagination.[2]

More importantly, it got me thinking about the power relationship between languages. Eventually, I would put some of these thoughts into my 1986 book, *Decolonising the Mind*. In the text,

2 See my memoir, *Wrestling with the Devil: A Prison Memoir* (New York: New Press, 2018).

I was really thinking of African languages and their unequal power relationship with imperial European languages. But I have since come to realize that the question of inequality of power between languages beleaguers the general assumptions about language relationships in the world today.

There are two ways by which different languages and cultures can relate to one another: as hierarchies of unequal power relationships (the imperial way), or as a network of equal give-and-take (the democratic way).

Silone could have made a case for translations without the invocation of the superiority of Italian over Bantu languages. That is the democratic way. For, in reality, there was everything to be gained from translation between Italian and English. It had been done before—in the Renaissance, English gained from translations from the Italian, for instance, from Boccaccio's work. But Silone did not embrace the democratic logic. For him, the proof of Italian equality to English lay in its being superior to Bantu languages. Silone's advocacy of more translations of the Italian into English was thus predicated on the assumption of hierarchy between languages and cultures. His case was clearly driven by imperial logic.

Unfortunately, the imperial logic has been the dominant in the relationship between languages. My language and culture are higher than your language and culture, sang all colonial systems as they set out to conquer and dominate and subjugate. The English did it in Ireland, Wales and Scotland; in America, Africa and Asia. Language conquest was the best way to help the English erase the memory of self-awareness among the Irish, wrote the poet Edmund Spenser as early as the 1590s, and so weaken their resistance to English settlement on their land.[3] A captain Pratt summed it up best when in 1892 he set up residency schools for the education of Native Americans, bragging later that the aim was to 'Kill the Indian [. . .] and save the man.'[4] Macaulay said the same when, in 1835, he advocated the use of English in India to replace Persian, to create a class of Indians who would be Indian in name, dress, colour of the skin, and even religion but with an English mindset.[5] The French started French-language institutions in their colonies to create a permanent psychological bond between their colonized elite and France. The Japanese tried the same in the case of their conquest and colonial occupation of Korea between 1910 and 1945: they imposed Japanese names and language on the Koreans. And of course the Spanish conquest of this part of the world, including Chile, went hand in hand with a systematic suppression of native languages, even deliberately burning books written in Native American languages; in the case

---

3 Edmund Spenser, *A Vewe of the Presente State of Ireland* (Manuscript, 1596; first printed edition, Dublin: James Ware, Society of Stationers, 1633).

4 Richard H. Pratt, 'The Advantages of Mingling Indians with Whites' [Text of speech delivered at an 1892 convention], *Americanizing the American Indians: Writings by the 'Friends of the Indian,' 1880–1900* (Cambridge, MA: Harvard University Press, 1973), pp. 260–71.

5 Thomas Babington Macaulay, 'Minute Upon Indian Education' (2 February 1835). In *Bureau of Education: Selections from Educational Records, Part I, 1781–1839* (H. Sharp ed.). Calcutta: Superintendent, Government Printing, 1920. Reprint: Delhi: National Archives of India, 1965, 107–17.

of the Maya, this resulted in putting to flames thousands of years of recorded history, philosophy and knowledge.

I was thinking of these fires when the day before yesterday I listened to the poem 'Fire' where the poet Veronica Zondek asks:

How can you swallow pain among blue flame
in the infernal burning at the stake of Inquisitions
or in the burning of books with Torquemada
or more recently,
Anguita,
when they incinerated books to suppress revolutions?[6]

The colonial system may not always have burnt books, but they did worse than incinerate: they attacked the very basis of knowledge production and storage.

In the colonial classroom, from Wales among the Welsh to New Zealand among the Māori people, the language of the dominated was associated with negativity, humiliation, and even violence. When some years ago, in 2008, I believe, the Welsh-language writer, Professor Angharad Price, author of *The Life of Rebecca Jones* (2014), received me at Bangor University in Wales, she recounted horror stories of Welsh kids being made to carry a sign that read 'WN / WELSH NOT' around their neck if caught speaking Welsh in the school compound. This was in nineteenth-century Wales; in twentieth-century colonial Kenya we were made

6 Verónica Zondek, *Cold Fire* (Katherine Silver trans.) (Storrs, CT: World Poetry Books, 2022).

to carry similarly humiliating items in addition to receiving corporal punishment.

In time, through gun, gore and guile, the monolingualism of the conqueror became the way, and today, it is a desirable norm in the making of nations. Worse is the normalization of that inequality in the minds of the elite of the hitherto dominated, even long after the formal attributes of domination have changed, as is the case in, say, postcolonial Africa.

In the continent, we spend millions of dollars to create a small class of perfect speakers of English, French or Portuguese, and deny knowledge to the majority of the population—speakers of African languages. We pamper European languages and pauperize African ones.

Yesterday, as I was going over this paper, I came across a link to a news item about a new law in Morocco: 'Morocco's legislators have adopted a new Education law that promotes the teaching of sciences in foreign languages, more so French. [. . .] [the] bill, Law 51.17 [. . .] stipulates the use of French as a language of instruction for scientific and technical subjects in Moroccan schools.'[7]

The implication is that neither Arabic nor Amazigh can be good enough for science and technology. Two ironies here. First, Arabic is a very rich language with a long history. After all it was Averroes—Ibn Rushd—an Arab scholar, who helped preserve Greek learning in the twelfth-century by writing many

7 See Maulline Gragau, 'Morocco's Controversial New Education Law Sparks Outrage', *The African Exponent* (23 July 2019). Available at: https://bit.ly/-3w5WcmA (last accessed on 16 August 2022).

commentaries on all aspects of classical Greek philosophy and science. Second, the same accusations of inadequacy were once made against French, English and other Western European languages as they emerged from the hegemony of Latin: that they cannot handle scientific and medical terms. Latin was then of course the language of imperial Rome.

In reality, there is no language, despite the number of its speakers, which is inherently more of a language than other languages. Every language is equally a memory bank of knowledge, information and experiences of the community that created it; and every language has the best and most detailed knowledge of the ecology of the area that produced it. Every language is equally capable of expansion to embrace new experiences, information and knowledge, even if they have to adopt words from other languages. Languages as mediums of information and knowledge can easily make new words or borrow from one another.

The word for table in Gĩkũyũ, is 'metha'. This is adopted from the Kiswahili 'meza'. This is taken from the Portuguese and Spanish 'mesa'. We have a few more: 'thabuni' for soap, adapted from the Kiswahili 'sabuni', adopted from the Portuguese or Spanish 'jabon'. We have adopted and naturalized many more terms from English. This is no different from other languages: most Western European languages have borrowed and naturalized many words and concepts from Latin and Greek.

But beyond lexical attributes, every language has its unique musicality which can never be replaced by another. In that sense, languages are like musical instruments.

There is no musical instrument which is inherently more a musical instrument than any other; the piano is not more of a musical instrument than, say, the violin or the guitar. Each has its unique musicality. You don't say: let us destroy all the other instruments and just have the piano. Arranged in a system of give-and-take, different instruments can form an orchestra and generate harmony. But the same group instruments arranged in a different order, in a hierarchy, becomes a catastrophe and produces cacophony.

The same is true of languages: arranged in a hierarchy of unequal power relationships—the imperial way—they produce catastrophe. Monolingualism, setting itself on top of the hierarchy, suffocates the subordinate languages and cultures. But arranged in a network of equal give-and-take—the democratic way—languages give life to each other. To sum up: monolingualism is the carbon monoxide of cultures; multilingualism is the oxygen.

Translation is one of the means by which languages and cultures do and can give life to each other. They enable the network of equal give and take—the democratic way.

I am not arguing a new case for translations. The facts speak for themselves. All world cultures have been impacted by translations. The Bible is probably the most translated text in history and has affected, for good or bad, the lives of millions. As have many other religious texts. European languages emerging from Latin hegemony during the European Renaissance benefitted a lot from translations from Latin and Greek. The thoughts of Marx ignited political and philosophical debates, revolutions even, all over the world, but these debates were based on translations from the German.

In my case, it was translations that connected me to Latin American literatures. The earliest I recall was a story we read in elementary school way back in the rural countryside of Kenya, about a man, his son and a donkey, who, out of contradictory advice from passers-by, end up carrying the donkey on their shoulders. Recently I bought a Spanish reader and found the same story now titled: '¿Padre hijo o caballo?'[8] in which father and son, out of their hearkening to contradictory advice from people, 'llegan al Mercado, pues, con el caballo en sus hombres [. . .]'.[9] The Spanish version is attributed to Don Juan Manuel, a writer from the Middle Ages. I suspect the Gĩkũyũ version, with the donkey replacing the horse, came from an English translation of the Spanish original. So, here, a chain of translations connected medieval Spain to twentieth-century Kenya.

In our struggles against the dictatorship in Kenya in the 1970s, we turned to Latin American poetry for inspiration—for instance, to the poetry of the Guatemalan Otto René Castillo: 'Intelectuales apoliticos' ('Apolitical Intellectuals').[10] When, in

---

8 Don Jon Manuel, '¿Padre hijo o caballo?' [Father, Son or Horse?] in Angel Flores (ed.), *First Spanish Reader: A Beginner's Dual-Language Book* (New York: Dover Publications, 1988), pp. 2–5.

9 Manuel, '¿Padre hijo o caballo?', p. 5: 'So, father and son arrive at the market with the horse on their shoulders [. . .]'.

10 Otto René Castillo, 'Intelectuales Apoliticos / Apolitical Intellectuals' (Margaret Randall trans.), *Berkeley Journal of Sociology* 20 (1975–76): 8–11.

1982, I came to writing my prison memoir, *Wrestling with the Devil*, I found a poem by yet another Latin American, a poet from Paraguay, Victor Jacinto Flecha, 'It's No Use', describing the circumstances around my arrest on the midnight of 31 December 1977.[11]

The impact of translation on most cultures is there for all to see. The case I am making is for the democratic way, the network of equal give-and-take to counter the imperial logic of hierarchy. This means pressuring all our governments and international institutions to change their policies and attitudes towards language, to reject the dictatorship of monolingualism. This means governments put resources into all the languages within their territories. Every language has a right to be. And as I have said: multilingualism gives oxygen to cultures.

We can then use translations as a way of ensuring conversations between and among languages. I have often described translation as the common language of languages. So let there be conversations among languages: first among the marginalized. I would like to see more translations between African languages, Asian and native South and North American languages. I would love to see translations between Mapudungun of the Mapuche or the Quechua of Chile and my own mother tongue, Gĩkũyũ, and other African languages. I mourn for the languages we have let die with all the knowledge they carried, all the musicality, buried

11 Victor Jacinto Flecha, 'It's No Use' (Nick Calstor trans.) in *Radical Arts Group Programme of Revolutionary Poetry* (Zaria, Nigeria: Ahmadu Bello University, 1983), p. 9.

with them. And, of course, translations between the formerly marginalized and the formerly marginalizing—between African, Asian and European languages—with translations seen as conversation. A conversation, as opposed to commands or exhortations, assumes equality among the interlocutors. Another way of thinking about it is translations as bridges: remember, there is never a one-way bridge.

I commend this conference, the organizers and the hosts; the Interdisciplinary Center of Studies in Philosophy, Arts, and Humanities, University of Chile. This is one more effort at enabling a global conversation among languages. I have just come from the Manchester International Festival in the UK, where a group, Studio Créole, organized a performance reading of stories written in Arabic, Croatian, Japanese, French, Icelandic, Spanish and Gĩkũyũ. Writers read their stories in the original language of composition, while being live-translated by an interpreter into English, and the rough English version was then fed via an earpiece to an actor, who smoothed out and acted out the translation. Meanwhile, every member of the audience was wearing a set of bone-conduction headphones, which meant that the audience could at the same time hear the original language and also the actor's English translation. I was proud to have participated in the performance with my story, 'Nyambura, Nyamĩcore na Mukungambura'.

According to Adam Thirlwell, one of the curators of the Studio Créole, their 'thinking was to make the relationship between literature and translation exposed and live and dramatic. As well as be some kind of festival of language, an act of resistance to any language (English, for instance) trying to assert itself as absolute and hegemonic.'[12]

I would like to cite one more project that exemplifies the effort to bring languages, big and small, into conversation through translations: the Jalada Translation Project.

In November 2015, a group of young writers who call themselves a Pan-African Writers' Collective, through their spokesperson, Munyao Kilolo, and through my son, Mũkoma, asked me to write for them an original story in Gĩkũyũ for their online journal *Jalada*. They wanted to release a translation issue, featuring especially African-to-African translations. I gave them the only story I had ready at the time: 'Ituĩka Rĩa Mũrũngarũ: Kana Kĩrĩa Gĩtũmaga Andũ Mathiĩ Marũngiĩ'—'The Upright Revolution: Or, Why Humans Walk Upright'.[13] By April 2016, the story had been translated into 30 languages. By now it has been translated into more than 90 languages in the world, including a native Mexican language.

12 See Manchester International Festival, 'Meet the Studio Créole Authors'. Available at: https://bit.ly/3zSnG04 (last accessed on 16 August 2022).

13 Ngũgĩ wa Thiong'o, 'Ituĩka Rĩa Mũrũngarũ: Kana Kĩrĩa Gĩtũmaga Andũ Mathiĩ Marũngiĩ', *Jalada* (22 March 2016). Available at: https://bit.ly/-3JXvWAI (last accessed on 6 April 2022). The story was subsequently published in the author's own English translation as an illustrated edition: *The Upright Revolution: Or, Why Humans Walk Upright* (Sunandini Banerjee ill.) (London: Seagull Books, 2019).

It is wonderful to see so many languages of the world, with their different scripts, conversing with one another through this one story—making the act of translation a language of languages!

Finding Our Way

Dialogue among Our Languages Is the Way to the Unity of African Peoples

This is a great day, and for me, as an African and as a writer, it is certainly one of the happiest days of my life. I began writing novels, short stories, plays and essays in 1960, when I was a student of English at Makerere University, Uganda, then an affiliate of the University College London. One can easily calculate and see that I have been wielding a pen for at least forty years.

From 1960 to 1977 I wrote in English even though all these books were mostly about Kenya and Kenyan people. But from 1977 to the present, I have written my novels, short stories, plays, and books for children in Gĩkũyũ, one of more than thirty African languages in Kenya. Half my writing life, then, was taken up with English, and the other half with Gĩkũyũ.

During that forty-year period, the conferences on African writing in English to which I have been invited have been many

---

This is an English translation from Gĩkũyũ of the keynote speech given at the conference 'Against All Odds: African Languages and Literatures into the 21st Century', held in Asmara, Eritrea, 11 January 2000.

and even the ones I have actually attended, starting with the famous 1962 Conference of African Writers of English Expression at Makerere, are countless. Now, in the same period, except for one at the School of Oriental and African Studies (SOAS) in London, I have never been invited to, or even heard about, a conference called for the sole purpose of discussing literature in African languages. This means that since the 60s of the last century—when African countries started gaining their independence—European languages have become the ones setting the terms of the debate on the literature of the continent. In schools and colleges in Africa and abroad, the literature which is taught under the label of African Literature is still mostly written in European languages. All the conferences to which I was invited were about African literature. A writer in any one African country could have been writing solely in an African language for any number of years without ever being heard outside the country. But let another person in the same country write and publish just one novel in English or French, and she begins to receive invitations to numerous conferences on African literature. Soon she becomes the representative of literature from that country and enters the curriculum. Thus, European languages also determine who is an African writer and who writes for Africa.

The situation of the European and African languages vis-à-vis the continent reminds me of a story I first read in Jomo Kenyatta's book *Facing Mount Kenya*.[1] The story is about a house, a man and

1 Jomo Kenyatta, *Facing Mount Kenya* (London: Mercury Books, 1961 [1938]), pp. 47–52. This is Kenyatta's rendering of the story of the Arab and his camel.

an elephant. The man is inside his hut, and the elephant is outside. The elephant first asks the man to be allowed to put his head inside the hut, then his legs and eventually his whole body, and once entirely inside he tells the man that there is not enough room for both of them. In the end the elephant is the one on the inside and the man on the outside—outside his former hut. It is the elephant who now tells the story of the hut and it seems as if everybody wants to hear about the hut more from the elephant than from the man who it. European languages have become like that elephant, and they often dictate the space which used to be occupied by African languages. They own the homestead otherwise called African literature.

As far as I know, and I stand to be corrected, this is the first conference on African soil, and probably the second in the world, to bring together in one place African writers and world scholars to discuss the present and the future of scholarship, literature and knowledge in African languages. That alone would still make me say that this is a great day and a happy occasion. I am happy to be part of this vast presence from the different parts of the continent and from the Caribbean and America. How inspiring that, despite her doctor's orders to rest, Nawal El Saadawi of Egypt stirred herself from bed, together with her partner Sherif Hetata, and came here to close ranks with the rest of the continent. I have always hated the division of Africa into one below the Sahara and another above it or one which is francophone and others which are lusophone or anglophone. We are here at the call of Afrophones.

Let me tell you a story. A long time ago, two young men, Muceru and Muiruri, were dressing up for a dance festival. Meceru told Muiruri: the clothes you are wearing don't fit you well, and they are certainly not suitable for the occasion. How can you go to such a festival without being dressed in a suit and tie? Muiruri started having doubts about his own clothes. Indeed, the more he now looked at himself, the more shabby his clothes seemed to be, especially when compared with the designer suits worn by his friend. Muiruri borrowed a suit and a matching tie from his friend. Muiruri was very proud of his new attire and he showed this by the way he walked: with a touch of arrogance, since it seemed to him that he carried the clothes even better than the original owner. On his arrival at the arena, every lady wanted to dance with him. Soon he felt hot, unbuttoned his shirt at the collar and loosened the tie to air his neck. Muiruri was in the middle of another dance when he saw Meceru approach and whisper to him, loudly enough for the dancing partner to hear: this tie that I loaned you is one of my finest and it does not look good worn so loose. Meceru even proceeded to tighten it a little. This did not amuse Muiruri and he now went to a different part of the arena. But now, while still enjoying dances with other partners, he kept making sure that the tie did not become lose again. Further, he kept looking over his shoulder, in case his benefactor turned up to embarrass him. That was how they spent the day—with Muiruri trying to keep up the sartorial expectations of his friend and at the same time trying to avoid his friend's cat-like vigilance. Muiruri relaxed only when the dance was over and they sat down to the banquet. Once again Muiruri was the object of admiration from the ladies. Then came the time for coffee. Suddenly Meceru raised his voice again: please be careful and don't spill coffee on the suit I loaned you. It is very expensive. I can even show you the receipt. Out of this story came the cautionary proverb: borrowed jewellery tires the wearer, for the owner will always find ways of hinting and drawing people's attention to the fact of his ownership.

This is how the *Observer,* one of London's major Sunday newspapers, greeted the 1965 production of Wole Soyinka's play *The Road* at the Commonwealth Arts Festival: '[. . .] a Nigerian called Wole Soyinka has done for our napping language what brigand dramatists from Ireland have done for centuries: booted it awake, rifled its pockets and scattered the loot into the middle of next week.'[2] The newspaper was saying this in praise of Wole Soyinka but there is a way in which it was also reminding him, along with all the writers of the famous Anglo-Irish tradition who had abandoned Gaelic with such enriching results for English, that they were welcome to add to the language but it was certainly not theirs.

You will remember how Prospero in the oft-quoted *The Tempest* told Caliban: when I first met you, you did not even know yourself, you spoke gibberish, but I gave you language and made you.[3] Instead of Caliban protesting and affirming that he

---

2 Penelope Gilliatt, 'Nigeria hits the London stage', *Observer* (19 September 1965). Available at: https://bit.ly/3pv1xjO (last accessed on 13 June 2022).

3 'I pitied thee, / Took pains to make thee speak, taught thee each hour / One thing or other: when thou didst not, savage, / Know thine own meaning,

did have a language prior to Prospero's presence on the island, Caliban demonstrates how well he can curse in the language.[4] Margaret Thatcher used to cite the spread of English to all parts of the world as evidence of the unique character of the English.[5]

We have not come here in order to argue whether or not we should be writing in African languages; we have not come here to argue as to whether or not African languages have adequate vocabularies; we have not come here to work out how we can best sing with other people's voices and still retain our own identities; we have not come here to debate as to how we can best use borrowed sounding systems or how we can claim them as ours. We are here in tune with the spirit of that saying that borrowed jewellery tires the wearer; and of another proverb which says that a man dances with his own kind, however small.

We have come to Asmara, Eritrea, driven by one hope: that even if it means stuttering with our tongues, we shall continue the struggle until we are able to sing sweetly in them; that we shall

---

but wouldst gabble like / A thing most brutish, I endow'd thy purposes / With words that made them known.' (William Shakespeare, *The Tempest* 1.2.353–58)

4 'You taught me language; and my profit on't / Is, I know how to curse. The red plague rid you / For learning me your language!' (*The Tempest* 1.2.362–64).

5 See, among others, Margaret Thatcher, 'The Language of Liberty: The Inauguration of the Thatcher Lecture Series', speech at the English-Speaking Union, New York, 7 December 1999. Available at: https://bit.ly/3Ac3O8m (last accessed on 20 August 2022).

step out in the arena and make the call: Mother, sing for me, for I shall one day come home victorious.

This day will be marked in the calendar of history as the day when African languages from different parts of the continent came together to reassert their historical right to being the spokestongues of Africa. It is the day the languages came together to say: We are products of Africa and we are producers of Africa. Africa gave us languages and we are going to use them to sing of Africa. In short, the languages of Africa have met here in Asmara to say: The homestead called African literature belongs to us all, and we, the different African languages, are brothers and sisters, children of one parent—Africa. From this day on, whenever two or more African languages meet, they will not be doing so in hostility but in comradeship. When one of the languages calls out in song:

> Whose homestead is this?
> Whose homestead is this?
> Whose homestead is this?
> So that I may dance with abandon
> Like we used to dance.

The other can answer back with pride:

> This homestead belongs to us all,
> This homestead belongs to us all,
> This homestead belongs to us all,
> If you want to dance with abandon,
> Do so like we used to dance.

A homestead is very important in all world communities. A home is not just a house. A home is the house and its total environment—the hedges, the trees, the cattle boma, the granaries, the yard, the shrines—and the activities which go on in those spaces. The other thing about a home is the *way* leading in and out of the homestead. The way which starts from the homestead is what eventually links that homestead to others, to the village, to the region, to the country and to the world. 'May you walk in the middle of the path' was how one was blessed at the start of a journey. Here, the way quite clearly means more than a physical entity.

Today's Africa, in both its positive and negative aspects, is a product of European colonialism and the struggles of African peoples against it. Colonialism was essentially a process of taking over a people's homestead and of taking people away from their way. The homestead is a person's base and colonialism can be seen as a process of alienating people from their total environment—their base and their way. The environment could be economic: the settler did not bring lands into Africa nor did he bring in labour. He seized the lands and then grew coffee, tea and mined precious metals with the labour of those whose land he had already taken. When these raw materials were processed in Europe, they became available to Africa at high prices. What about the political environment? The colonizer did not bring an army from Europe: he made armies out of the divisions between African peoples and he helped set community against community, region against region, clan against clan, and they all ended up being alienated from their power base while the colonizer became empowered. They used our power to get power and then used the power against us all.

One of the most serious was the alienation from the cultural environment. The cultural environment is what carries the way, a people's way, into the world. The way is what tells people who they are. And the way is also what leads people into their collective homestead. To alienate a people from their way is to deprive the people of the power to connect with the world and their base. The way is carried by language. The quickest means of achieving the alienation of a people from the way and from their power base, then, is through language.

In the eighteenth century, a certain slave owner in Virginia, William Lynch, wrote to fellow slave owners on how to break the resistance of the slaves. And it is interesting how he quickly zeroed in on language as the most effective way of lynching the mind and the body of the enslaved. 'We must completely annihilate the mother tongue of both the new nigger and the new mule,' he said, 'and institute a new language that involves the new life's work of both.' Create a mule out of a nigger through language. The loss of language would inevitably lead to the loss of any connection with one's history and worldview. The experts, William Lynch went on, say that 'the mind has a strong drive to correct and re-correct itself over a period of time if it can touch some substantial original historical bases and they advise that the best way to deal with this phenomenon is to shave off the brute's mental history and create a multiplicity of phenomenon or illusions.'[6] Is this essentially different from the words of Macaulay when he spoke of English in Indian colonial education as a means of creating a class of natives Indian in colour but with an English mind, so that the class would create a buffer zone between the colonizing minority and the colonized majority? In both cases, they are talking about lynching the mind of the enslaved so as to create a multiplicity of illusions, even about their own bodies and environment.[7] Alienation from one's total environment brings the disease called Not-Knowing-Oneself. Those who do not know themselves are like persons drugged by alcohol. They can be turned any way without any resistance, and William Lynch understood that quite clearly.

The struggle for independence was a struggle for a people to be in control of their entire environment. But something went wrong at the raising of the flag. Or rather, by the time we came to raise the flag, we found that the mind of the elite had been lynched—they had lost the way into the homestead and had become like those talked of in the Bible: seeing, they do not see; hearing; they do not hear.[8]

---

6 William Lynch, *The Willie Lynch Letter: The Making of a Slave* (Bensenville, IL: Lushena Books, 1999). The historical accuracy of the story is contested. But whether real or not, it illustrates the point.

7 I have discussed the connection between language and the other realms of our being in my book *Decolonising the Mind* (Portsmouth, NH: Heinemann, 1986).

8 Matthew 13:13; Mark 8:18.

Let me give a few examples to illustrate the blindness of those who have eyes but fail to see and the deafness of those who have ears but fail to hear because of the multiplicity of illusions implanted in their minds by colonial Willie Lynch.

Africa is one of the richest continents in the world but Africa is one of the poorest continents in the world. Africa spends a huge percentage of its national income on education. But a hundred percent of the knowledge thereby generated ends up hidden in European languages. And yet it is the majority of African people who most need that knowledge. Why can't we put all that knowledge into African languages instead of the current practice of hiding it in European ones?

Another example. We know that our real strength lies in the unity of Africa and African peoples. If Africa was united today, it would become one of the most powerful entities in global affairs. In each of our countries, it was the unity of the various nationalities which made possible the achievement of independence. The spirit of unity guided us and we talked of pan-African unity. It was Europe which used to laugh at our dreams of the unity of African peoples. But look at our situation today. When European countries are uniting to the extent of even having a common parliament, a common currency and a common passport, we in Africa are doing the exact opposite: erecting as many barriers as possible to the movement of peoples and goods across our national frontiers; and at times retreating into ethnic enclaves and even splitting along clan lines.

The mention of unity brings me to the question which I am asked most often whenever I talk about writing in African languages: Writing in our languages—won't that actually deepen ethnic divisions?

It is true that in each African country there are many nationalities and they speak different languages. But we should not hide our heads in the sand like the celebrated ostrich and pretend that this is not so or that we can solve the problems of that reality by importing a language of national salvation from Europe. There was a time when humans used to think of seas, oceans, gravity and space as barriers and enemies until they learnt how to use them. Why then not pose the question of multiplicity of languages and nationalities differently? We should ask: How can the many languages be used to bring about the unity of African peoples within a country and within Africa?

Let me start with the continent. There are two ways of bringing about African unity. The colonial boundaries, the basis of the present nation states in Africa, often divided a people with the same history, language and culture into different territories. Thus, we may find a group of nation states actually sharing the same people. The best-known example is that of the Somali people split five ways so that some belong to Kenya and others to Ethiopia, Djibouti and the Somali Republic. There are Maasai people in both Kenya and Tanzania. Similarly, the Oromo people are both in Kenya and in Ethiopia. This pattern is repeated in all Africa. The question is this: Why can't we use these shared communities as the practical and moral basis of unity between our countries?

Under this scenario, the Maasai people would then become a uniting force between Tanzania and Kenya, for instance. Equally well the Somali people could become the bridgeheads of unity between Djibouti, Somalia, Kenya and Ethiopia. The Oromo people would cement the same unity by virtually nullifying the boundary between Kenya and Ethiopia. The pattern is the same from South to North Africa, from East to West Africa, and if this pattern was followed through, the shared communities would bring the entire continent together and thus turn colonial boundaries, meant to bring about divisions and weaknesses, into their opposites: bridgeheads of unity and strength. In short, we turn the shared communities and languages into links of the chain of African unity. This is obviously a matter of politics and political will and it is mostly in the hands of those wielding state power. But even here there can be grassroots pressure.

The second way—and it does not conflict with the first—is to let our languages dialogue with one another. In practical terms this means developing literature and knowledges in these languages, while at the same time encouraging translations of works into the different languages. A novel or a story written in Tigrinya could be translated into Tigre, Saho, Afar within, say, Eritrea, but even across Eritrea into Amharic, Kiswahili, Ibo, Yoruba, Chichewa and Zulu. This means that children of the different nationalities would read and often identify with stories, characters, names and actions set in a different region. In time, a child of one nationality may come to feel that he knows the characters and names of a different nationality almost as well as he knows those of his immediate neighbourhood. This also creates respect for the language and culture that produced such wonderful stories and situations. In time, the children in one country would find that their languages share a common culture and heritage. The same would be true of the continent as a whole. This would surely create a good and solid cultural foundation for the country and for Africa. Translations and the learning of more than one African language would be built into the school and university curricula.

The dialogue of African languages in this conference at Asmara, Eritrea, is therefore very important in its own right, but also in showing the directions in which African languages can grow and enhance our unity. Thus, the fact that we are gathered here at all calls for celebration.

Indeed, we have come here to celebrate the fact that African languages have overcome so many odds. They have been despised, made invisible in their own land and in world affairs, but they refuse to be buried alive, they still survive. In this respect, it is fortunate that this pioneering meeting has been held in this country and this region, where there has been a demonstrable continuity of written languages—from the ancient Sabaean and Ge'ez with their origins in the pre-Christian era to the present Tigrinya and other languages in Eritrea and Ethiopia that claim connections with those ancient languages. We are here to celebrate that continuity as an inspiration for the future of African languages. We are here to celebrate all the writers who have tirelessly kept faith with our languages and made that continuity possible.

But even though we are here to celebrate we must, along with it, accept the challenges first of creating a modern literature and modern systems of knowledge in our languages and then making the same available in our different languages. We have to create literature and knowledge which speak to the most urgent needs of our people for economic and political survival. This can only be achieved through a collective effort and alliances within our countries. Let me mention a few.

There is, first and foremost, the position of the various governments. African governments have to come up with progressive policies on language matters. One of the things which often stand in the way of adequate policies for African languages is the false logic of monolingualism and particularly the notion of one national language which has to swallow up all the others. A variation of this is the assumption that only the languages of the big ethnic groups can become regional and national. Every language whether spoken by a community of hundreds or by a community of millions has a right to exist and a right to develop literature and knowledge unhindered by the policies of the state. The acceptance of the unqualified equality of all the nationalities within any one country and in Africa as a whole is the prerequisite for any success of a national or even a continental language policy. If in the course of time and in practice there emerges one language which serves the needs of communication in the entire nation or region, this would be a positive development. Here we have the example of Kiswahili in East Africa. But this should not mean the active or even passive destruction of the other languages. This position is based on a simple premise. If we believe that people are the basis of development, then the language or languages that they speak are the basis of that progress and every language policy and planning should incorporate this premise. African states must also realize that the development of African languages will seriously be hindered unless there is freedom of expression of differences. Debates and even differences of thought and the clash of opposing ideas are the basis of genuine development of a healthy society. African languages must be at the frontline in the discovery and invention of knowledge in the arts, in the sciences and technology and this kind of renaissance is impossible if people are scared of saying what is in their minds and of concern to their hearts. In my view democracy is the best foundation for adequate state policies on language. In looking at the emerging language policies in Eritrea and South Africa, I feel enormously encouraged.

Publishers are a very important ingredient in the renaissance of African languages. We need publishers who have faith in the possibilities of our languages. We need commercial publishers willing to invest in the production of books in African languages. In this respect, we note with pride that one of the most important forces behind this conference is Africa World Press. I believe very strongly that there is an untapped market for books in African languages and it is likely to be an ever-expanding market. If an adequate readership develops in any African language, then that readership will also be the one most ready to consume books translated from other languages. Publishers in one region can exchange materials with those from other regions.

Scholars, whether from Africa or outside Africa, are another important ingredient, for they will also pose questions and conduct research on the products of these languages and thus help to set standards. It is a welcome sight to see so many scholars from all over the world who will forever be part of this historic day.

Thus, the development of African languages should not mean isolation from other languages of the earth. There is a lot that African languages can learn from those of Europe, Asia and Latin America. African languages must open themselves out particularly to the heritage of those Africans who have now built new nations and communities in the Caribbean, America and in the Pacific. What has been produced by Langston Hughes, George Lamming, Aimé Césaire, Margaret Walker, Amiri Baraka, Sonia Sanchez, Toni Morrison is part of our heritage and it should be accessible to communities within Africa in their own languages. We have to build bridges to those that Kamau Brathwaite has termed 'nation languages' in the Caribbean. All the great works in European languages should be available in our languages. This means that in addition to our languages holding dialogues among themselves they must open dialogues with the other languages of the earth. We want African languages to become bridgeheads to continental African unity and to pan-African unity. But we also want them to shake hands with all human languages. Let our languages be our way into humanity's search and struggle for democracy and social justice and a spiritual culture which measures progress not in terms of those on the mountaintop but in terms of those whom Frantz Fanon identified as the 'Wretched of the Earth'.

With all that, then, I believe that the biggest challenge is still to writers and intellectuals of Africa. We have to leave this meeting determined to do more for our languages and in our languages. I have said before and I say it again that we must do for our languages what all other intellectuals have done for theirs by producing the best that can be written and thought. Let us therefore make sure that when we leave Asmara we shall be armed with a united vision of new beginnings. May this conference be the beginning of greater things to come for our languages, for Africa, for the world? Thaai.

Translation, Restoration and a Global Culture

I am not a translator; or, rather, my experience in the field is in auto-translation from Gĩkũyũ to English. I did my own translation of my first-ever novel in Gĩkũyũ, *Caitani Mũtharabainĩ* (1980), published in English under the title *Devil on the Cross* (1982), and then *Mũrogi wa Kagogo* (2005) as *Wizard of the Crow* (2006). With my co-author Ngũgĩ wa Mĩriĩ, we translated our play *Ngaahika Ndeenda* (1980), which was published under the title *I Will Marry When I Want* (1982). I have also tried my hand at translating from English into Gĩkũyũ. Although I don't have many years' work in translation, my seven years' work as director of the International Center for Writing and Translation at the University of California–Irvine made me become more conscious of the role of translation in our history and social being.

Translation has been part of my life. The first book I've ever read as a neo-literate, way back in the late forties of the last century, was a torn copy of stories culled from the Old Testament. It was in Gĩkũyũ, my mother tongue, and it was only years later that I learned that it was a translation put together by Christian missionaries. The translation was also, almost certainly, from the

English-language Bible, itself a translation from the Greek and the Hebrew originals, themselves translations from the many tongues, Aramaic included, that the various biblical characters must have spoken in real, historical life. So the founding text of my literary culture was a translation of a translation of several translations. Not that I was aware of it then, but even if I had been, it wouldn't have worried me in the least. I found the stories interesting, and my only concern was the fact that the pages were literally falling apart. I was happy when years later I was able to own a copy of the whole Bible, again in Gĩkũyũ. The Bible as a translation is a founding text of modern Gĩkũyũ-language prose, and it has played a similar role in many literary-national traditions. The entire Christian world community is able to realize itself through translation, as I'm sure the Muslim world through the Koran's translations, not just literally and religiously, but also socially; and it is not too far-fetched to say that even human society itself, religious or not, is founded on the practice of translation.

In *The German Ideology*, young Marx and Engels see the entire but complex process by which humans act on nature to produce their means of life as a language, or what they call 'the language of real life', meaning the practice by which humans take from the language of nature and put that learning to their own use.[1] That's

1 Karl Marx and Friedrich Engels, 'Idealism and Materialism' in 'Feuerbach: Opposition of the Materialist and Idealist Outlooks' in *The German Ideology* (Moscow: Progress Publishers, 1968). Available at: https://bit.ly/3CgDQDz (last accessed on 13 June 2022).

translating knowledge from one environment—in this case *natural*—in terms of another, the *nurtural*. Humans translate the language and the laws of nature into those of nurture. Humans are of nature, like plants, animals, air, say ecology, and yet they stand outside it, as it were, act on it and reproduce themselves, and give rise to processes, which are clearly not identical with the nature of which they are part. And yet, what humans have achieved is an extension of the various aspects of nature. The most wonderful technological tools are an extension of the human hand. The farthest-seeing telescope is an extension of the eye, as are the speediest vehicles—rockets and spaceships, for instance—extensions of the leg, the act of walking. And the computers—don't they try to imitate the human brain? So the translation of the language of nature into their own tongues has enabled humans to create their nurture out of nature. The nurtural world of the human is an endless reproduction of what obtains in the *natural* nature, and even the word 'cultivate' gives rise to the concept of culture as a social practice. Agriculture and social culture have a common root in the notion of cultivating nature, itself a process of translation from one environment to another.

In short, the humanization of nature is itself a process of translation and bespeaks of the centrality of translation in the make-up of our human community. Aristotle said that poetry was more universal than history since history dealt with the particulars while poetry dealt with what could be. But there is a way in which we can say that the subject of translation is the universals contained in the particulars of natural and social experience.

Every phenomenon of nature, society and human thought contains its own particularity, its form that gives it individuality. But embedded in it is an element of the universal: the two—the particular and the universal—are an integral part of each other. The universality in phenomena is expressed through its particularity. Thus, an individual human being has their particularity in terms of height, weight, shape of face, colour, but they also contains the universal that we call human. The capacity to speak language as organized sounds, to express meaning is universal to all humans; however, it does not express itself in its universality but in its particularity, as specific languages spoken by different peoples. In the same way, the universals of the twin struggles with nature and with one another are expressed in the particularities of different languages and cultures. Translations take the universal in one particularity to express it in another particularity. If you like, it disrobes or divests the universal of its particular linguistic robes, so to speak, to give it new robes. That's why it enables contact. But in other words, if there is nothing at all in common between two particularities, absolutely nothing, translation becomes impossible. So it is the universality of phenomena that enables translation of the particulars. But at the same time, in practice and in theory, it is a complex process, simultaneously an imitation, an expression of identity, difference, addition, interpretation and reproduction, and that's why no two translations can be the same, or rather they are the same insofar as they touch on the universal they are trying to convey, and they are different because conveyed in particularities, coloured by different experiences and outlooks for the individual and the collective. That's why, in so many ways, a translation is really a new work—a work of art. What comes out of it is really a work which is not quite identical with the original. It is a new work. Translators in our society should be better acknowledged. Translation is a creative process in its own right and translators are creative interpreters because a part of their own soul is contained in the new work, in the new translated work.

Not surprisingly, translation with all its contradictions is noted in both myth and history. In Plato's *Cratylus*, Hermes is referred to as signifying that 'he is the interpreter, or messenger, or thief, or liar or bargainer' (408a–b). Translator as a liar? A thief? All those contraries do apply to the act and process of translations because it is decidedly not a neutral process. Not only do particularities differ, but the very context of their production and application, whether of equality or of ordination and subordination, conditions the uses, negative or positive, to which they are put, and they may become messengers of healing, robbing, or distorting. Translations can be agents of equal or unequal exchange and this is borne out by the uses to which translation has been put in history.

In his book, *The Hellenic Philosophy: Between Europe, Asia and Africa*, Christos C. Evangeliou talks movingly and analytically of the historical interaction between peoples and cultures of those regions around the Mediterranean, particularly between the ancient Hellenes and Egyptians, and at one point quotes Herodotus as saying that the cooperation between the Ionian Greeks and the Egyptians began at the reign of Psammetichus I, who, in response to the help he got from the Ionians in defeating his enemies, granted them land and gold and silver, and 'even went so far as to put some Egyptian boys in their charge to be taught Greek; and their learning of the language was the origin of the class of Egyptian interpreters'.[2] Here translation is seen as helping in cementing the relations between two cultures on the basis of mutual aid, respect and acceptance.

That was in times of cooperation, but of course in times of mutual strife, even among the hitherto friendly and cooperative, translation can and does play the role of reproducing the culture of domination and submission, and colonialism provides a good example. In my book *Penpoints, Gunpoints and Dreams*, I have cited another instance in the fifteenth- and sixteenth-century contact between Western Europe and West Africa in which Africans were lured into English ships, taken to England, where they were taught English and thus later provided as translators/interpreters for English explorers, the forerunners of slave raiders.[3] In fact, translation and interpretation have been an integral part of the colonial enterprise from its beginning stages as exploration and conquest to its later stages as occupation, settlement and control. Not surprisingly, the character of the translator/interpreter is a most satirized figure in anti-colonial narratives where he is often

2 Herodotus, *Histories* 2.154, quoted in Christos C. Evangeliou, *The Hellenic Philosophy: Between Europe, Asia and Africa* (Binghamton: Binghamton University, 1997)

3 Ngũgĩ wa Thiong'o, *Penpoints, Gunpoints and Dreams: Towards a Critical Theory of the Arts and the State in Africa* (Oxford: Clarendon Press, 1998).

seen as a messenger of the foreign, a thief and a liar into the bargain, the celebrated mythical Hermes in colonial robes. But translations have also played a role in resistance and transformation, and I recall the terror that Marx's *Communist Manifesto* seemed to strike in the hearts of our colonial educators, who constantly warned against it, even though they had removed it from school and public libraries.

It is in fact during the colonial process that the relationships between languages become really distorted and translation becomes dictation from the dominant culture on the dominated culture. Just as in the realms of economics and politics, so in cultures, the world became divided into a handful of the dominant and hundreds of the dominated, a situation reflected in the relations between languages today. In more ways than one, the global world is an inheritor of global colonialism. A handful of languages literally dominate all the other languages of the globe. Some languages, with all the knowledge they contain, are even dying under the pressure for linguistic and cultural homogenization. The world of languages and cultures has thus become divided into a dominant few and a marginalized many. Whereas translation has been a two-way traffic among the dominant, it has become dictation between the marginalized and the dominant, with the dominant dictating the interflow, with the result that many intellectuals of the postcolonial world have abandoned their languages altogether to write, theorize and scholarize in the dominant. They may argue that they are using the borrowed dominant differently, and this is largely true, but the fact remains that at the end of the day, it is the these intellectuals' languages and cultures of the birth that have been deprived. The intellectuals may be excellent spokespeople of their own cultures through their mastery of the dominant. English may even give them a world stage to display the dynamism of their cultures. But this is a case of the dominant *enabling* while *disabling*. It enables such intellectuals and the cultures they represent to voice their originality, but it disables the voice of those cultures and languages by depriving them of some of their best minds and geniuses. And between the marginalized, almost total silence! There are hardly any mutual translations among let's say Gujarati, Yoruba, Igbo, Zulu and Native American languages.

And yet, given the speed of globalization and the tensions it is generating, the need for genuine dialogue among cultures and languages on the basis of equality and mutual respect has never been greater, and hence the need for translations as conversation as opposed to a one-way traffic or dictation. At the International Center for Writing and Translation (ICWT), we borrowed for an inspirational motto a line from Aimé Césaire's book *Discourse and Colonialism*, where he says that culture contact is the oxygen of civilization.[4] By enabling cultural contact and exchange, translation as conversation becomes a civilizing agency in the globe.

4 Aimé Césaire, *Discourse on Colonialism* (Joan Pinkham trans.) (New York: Monthly Review Press, 2000), p. 33: 'a civilization that withdraws into itself atrophies; that for civilizations, exchange is oxygen; that the great good fortune of Europe is to have been a crossroads, and that because it was the locus of all ideas, the receptacle of all philosophies, the meeting place of all sentiments, it was the best center for the distribution of energy.'

That is why I saw heading ICWT as both a challenge and a dream. The dream was contained in the ideals of a circle. If the globe is seen as a circle, then languages should be seen as occupying their place in the ring. The challenge is in creating a model for the practical or, rather, creating a paradigm for a model of a practice that enables the dream. Our aim was to encourage a model for conversation among languages, first of all among the marginalized themselves, as well as between the marginalized as a whole and the hitherto dominant. Our aim was to encourage the making visible, the genius even in the most marginalized of languages, while at the same time restoring genius to its original base.

In such a scenario, we can pose different questions and challenges to English and other dominant languages. Given the position history has thrust upon such languages, no matter how they came to occupy that position, we have to challenge them to enable without disabling. How can English enable, which it has been doing, but at the same time not disable, which it has also been doing? I think it is our role as translators to make this happen. We can use English to enable conversation where two languages are currently not able to converse directly. Works in Korean can be translated into Gĩkũyũ and vice versa with English enabling contact between Korean and Gĩkũyũ without necessarily disabling one or both. English and other languages similarly situated become mediators among several marginalized languages. I have translated two Molière plays, *Tartuffe* and *The Doctor in Spite of Himself*, into Gĩkũyũ but through the English translations. I have done the same with Nikolai Gogol's *The Government Inspector*.

But another way of enabling is what we at the ICWT call restoration. A lot of the intellectual production by the native keepers of memory in Asia, the Pacific and within North American Native populations has been in languages other than the ones of the cultures of their birth and upbringing. In reality, this is often an act of cultural translation from the subject memory into the dominant memory. But it is a mental act, which means that in the process the would-be-original text is lost. The restoration project imagined at the ICWT involved the support for models of translations for works written in dominant languages back to the original languages and cultures from which the writer had drawn. We call it a project of restoration because, in putting works back into the original languages (or into other marginalized languages) helps restore the work to its original culture without interfering in its existence in the dominant memory—almost like rescuing 'the original' mental text from exile. Conceived as a global project, it would affect quite a number of cultures in Asia, Africa, Europe and elsewhere, and it would help in reversing the brain drain by ensuring that the products of that brain drain go back to build the local base.

The success of such restoration would have to be a creative partnership among the writer, translator and publisher. Given the place that English occupies in the world today, it should be used to enable conversation among languages without disabling. We should explore ways of encouraging a pilot model for what should be a global restoration project, calling for a grand alliance of publishers, translators and financiers. This process has already started.

I understand that two or three of Wole Soyinka's plays have been translated into Yoruba. Many works by African writers have been translated into Kiswahili. In India, too, some of the works, Salman Rushdie's for instance, have been translated into Indian languages. This process, already underway and embraced by all, then becomes a conscious global project that can do a lot in democratizing the cultural space among the different languages and cultures in the world.

In both projects, translation is the key word. Translation becomes truly the language spoken by languages or, rather, the universal common oeuvre of languages. Translation theories and practices will help in maintaining the integrity of languages and cultures, while enabling them to share in each other's triumphs. All languages then should be seen as tributaries to the common sea of humanity. Translation should help in countering the dictatorship of monolingualism. Quite frankly, there is beauty, power and glory in many languages, but monolingualism has blinded nations into having a mono-view of reality.

Perhaps we could, or should, learn from nature. Take the flower, for instance. What is significant about the flower is that it is not only a very visible expression of a plant; it also contains the seeds for the future reproduction of the same plant. But flowers come in different colours, and we do not say that a flower is a flower only if it expresses itself in one colour. Even roses are not all red. This is of course also their attraction. But no flower can claim to be more of a flower than others, in that they all contribute to the celebration of beauty and the reproduction of life. Many languages do not devalue any one language—and in a world of many languages expressing our humanity, translation can, must and will play a most important role in enabling free and creative conversations among them, to the benefit of our collective civilization. Translators then become missionaries for the future of the global culture.

Encounters with Translation

A Globalectic View

In *Dreams in a Time of War* (2011), my memoir of childhood written in English, I have talked about the evening storytelling sessions by the fireside. One of the stories that left a mark in me was about a father, his son and their donkey, who on the way to the market try to live up to every opinion of neighbours and strangers as to who should carry whom. Father and son end up carrying the donkey on their shoulders. As Dennis Tedlock pointed out in his talk yesterday,[1] in some communities stories can only be told in the evening with the warning—not of snakes in our case but of the fact that stories vanished in daylight and appeared only at night.

Talk given at a conference on Literature and Global Culture: The Voice of the Translator, University of California, Santa Barbara, 24 January 2015.

1 Dennis Tedlock, 'The Palimpsest, the Mirror and the Collage', talk given at a conference on Literature and Global Culture: The Voice of the Translator, University of California, Santa Barbara, 23 January 2015.

Later when I learnt to read and write, I discovered, to my amazement, that I could tell myself stories without making the story fly away and hide. Well, they could not. They had been captured in books. Lo and behold, in my Gĩkũyũ-language primer, I encountered the same story, with the added pleasure of illustrations, including the depiction of the father and son, a donkey hanging from a pole on their shoulders, arriving at the market, with people looking at them in utter astonishment at their stupidity.

I discovered another secret. The storyteller in the evening must have oralized the story from its written form. No matter, it was the same story, part of my Gĩkũyũ cultural heritage. It is only last year in Irvine, when I started learning Spanish, that I made another discovery. It was a free translation and adaptation of the Spanish story, '¿Padre hijo o caballo?' by the medieval Spanish writer, Don Juan Manuel.[2] Only that in the Gĩkũyũ-language version, *el caballo*, the horse, becomes the donkey. But it is very unlikely that in colonial Kenya, there would have been anybody who knew Spanish. So the Gĩkũyũ version was probably a translation from the English or some other source. Whatever the sequence, my real encounter with written word in Gĩkũyũ was through translation. The same was true of my first encounter with the Bible in Gĩkũyũ: it was a translation of a series of translations—English, Latin, Greek, Hebrew, Aramaic all the

2 Don Jon Manuel, '¿Padre hijo o caballo?' [Father, Son or Horse?] in Angel Flores (ed.), *First Spanish Reader: A Beginner's Dual-Language Book* (New York: Dover Publications, 1988), pp. 2–5.

way back to the language that God, Adam and Eve used in the Garden of Eden.

This is not unique to Gĩkũyũ. The entire intellectual tradition in the West (indeed the very development of the now-dominant European languages) was impacted by translation. In the dominant religious systems of Islam and Christianity, both religions of the book, it was the translation of the book that enabled their spread all over the world. The translation of the Greek and Latin classics into English, French and German not only aided in the growth of the languages but also impacted the study of drama, poetry and philosophy.

This, obviously, is the positive side of translation. But there is the negative side. In the early part of the colonial era in Kenya, priests in Catholic churches conducted mass in Latin—this, despite the fact that the majority of their African adherents were regular folk, most of whom could not even read and write their African languages. The sound system of the priestly, sonorous words, 'Gloria, gloria in excelsior Deo' would come across as 'Ngururia Ngururia'. So the young folk rendered the priest as saying: 'Ngururia Ngururia na Ndũkangururĩrie mĩiguainĩ, Ngururĩria mĩrĩyoini ya ngwacĩ ndahũta thiĩ ngĩcirĩyagaaaa!' This translates roughly as 'drag me, but don't drag me along the field of thorns: drag me along a field of sweet potatoes so when I feel hungry, I can pick a few and eat . . .'

Here is a case of a sound-to-sound translation that clearly subverts the religious intent of the mass. A sound signifier is bound up in the culture and history of a community, and can only translate into another as nonsense. When the Greeks thought of foreigners as barbarians, those that made seemingly nonsensical sounds, they were responding to sound signifiers. Europeans reacted similarly to the sounds coming from the New World. In *The Tempest*, Shakespeare's Prospero accuses Caliban of having had no language prior to Prospero's conquest of Caliban's island.

In my recent talks and writings on the current Western metaphysical empires of language and culture, I have found it necessary to preface my remarks by referencing an article, 'L'Irlanda alla sbarra' [Ireland at the Bar] that James Joyce published in the Italian journal *Il Piccolo dell Sera* on 16 September 1907.[3]

'Ireland at the Bar' tells a story of four or five peasants from the village in Maamtrasna in western Ireland, arrested and accused of murdering a woman. The accused, among them a sixty-year-old, did not know English. The court resorted to the services of an interpreter to make the Gaelic-speaking accused heard. Asked if he had seen the woman on the morning in question, the bewildered sixty-year-old would go into lengthy explanations in Gaelic; the 'officious interpreter', however, would reduce the entire explanation into: 'He says no, your worship.' Asked if he was in the vicinity, the old man went through a similarly lengthy explanation; the interpreter reduced it to: 'He says no, your worship.' The man was sentenced to death and according to Joyce, 'Legend has it that even the hangman could not make himself understood by

3 James Joyce, 'Ireland at the Bar' (Conor Deane trans.) in *Occasional, Critical and Political Writing* (Kevin Barry ed.) (Oxford: Oxford University Press, 2000). Available at: https://bit.ly/3AA5Y3c (last accessed on 14 June 2022).

the victim and angrily kicked the unhappy man in the head to force him into the noose.'

Here translation both enables the legal proceedings and also subverts the intent of the judicial process. The accused are completely outside the entire process, yet they bear the full consequences of whatever decision is arrived at as a result of the arguments between the defence, the prosecution and the bench.

'Ireland at the Bar' brings out the differential power relations between Gaelic and English. But it could be describing a scene in any independent African nation today where the majority are similarly rendered linguistically deaf and mute by policies that have set European languages as the normative measure of worth in every aspect of national life: the majority depend on translation.

Here, translation may enable the functioning of the nation, but this constant translation takes place in the context of differential power relations between the language of conquest, as the national and official language, and the majority of native languages, as the victims of conquest. The majority's participation in the entire management of wealth, the administration of justice, the production of culture, is dependent on interpretation and translation. The fact is that the majority in Africa, or generally in the formerly colonized world, live as outsiders in the own country. Call them foreignized nationals. In short, the languages of the majority are marginalized to give the centre to languages spoken by a minority class.

How does a writer who comes from these marginalized languages negotiate their literary journey through such a terrain?

I want to use this occasion not to theorize; I have done enough of this in my books, *Decolonising the Mind, Something Torn and New* and *Globalectics*. I just want to share with you my encounters with translation.

I have already mentioned that translations were my initial reading material in Gĩkũyũ. But when eventually I came to write, I did what all my literary contemporaries were doing—write in English. But looking back on my English-language novels—*Weep not Child* and *The River Between* in particular—I can now see that writing them was an act of translation, a process I call mental translation. The characters I wrote about spoke Gĩkũyũ or Kiswahili in their everyday life. The history they made, they did using African languages. So whatever I made them say, especially when I wanted to capture the rhythms of speech and their nuances in English, it involved an act of translation.

Then in 1977, after publishing four novels in English, I decided to write directly in Gĩkũyũ. But I found it necessary to do a translation into English, for, even within Kenya, only one community speaks Gĩkũyũ. We are a multilingual nation. The problem would have been solved immediately if all the other African languages were equally thriving in publishing. Then it would have meant that the book would be available in all the forty languages. But that was not the reality. I translated my first novel in Gĩkũyũ, *Caitani Mũtharabainĩ*, into English as *Devil on the Cross.* This was my first attempt at auto-translation or author-translation. In this I was clearly influenced by the previous practice of mental translation: I tried to make the reader aware of the source language, its rhythms.

Matigari, my second novel in Gĩkũyũ, was translated by Wangui wa Goro into English. Her translation is concerned less with making the reader conscious of the source language than in making it flow in the target language while capturing the spirit of the novel. I translated my third novel in Gĩkũyũ, *Mũrogi wa Kagogo*, as *Wizard of the Crow*. Here I followed Goro's footsteps: I was more concerned with its flow in the target language. I argued that if anybody wanted to know how it felt in Gĩkũyũ, then they should read it in Gĩkũyũ. In my view, this process was the more faithful to the spirit of the original than was the case when I had tried to force the presence of the source into the target.

My difficulties in writing in Gĩkũyũ have not really come from the act of writing or the process of translating but, rather, from the publishers. I have about five to six manuscripts in Gĩkũyũ that have not yet found the light of publication. When the publisher accepts to publish in Gĩkũyũ, it is only with an eye to the English translation, to which they will then give all the attention. So ironically, translations into English, be it auto-translation or by another hand, has worked against my efforts in Gĩkũyũ. I now want to make sure that my next major works in Gĩkũyũ are *not* translated into English, until a specified period of time, say two or three years.

As for shorter works, the occasional essay, the short story, the poem, there are no magazines or newspapers to take them. I founded an online Gĩkũyũ journal, *Mũtiiri*, but even then, to get a committed administrator of the website has not been easy. So most of these are still among my computer files.

But now and then I do get a venue for publishing them: in English language magazines and newspapers. Here I use the English translation to enable my Gĩkũyũ language publication.

The practice started at Yale where I was visiting professor of English and comparative literature from 1989 to 1992. The young scholars around the *Yale Journal of Criticism*, among them Professor David Marshall, asked me to contribute. I told them that I wrote in Gĩkũyũ. They said why not? They would publish my paper but I would have to provide an English translation. I agreed on the condition that the original and the translation would not be published side by side but, rather, as two independent papers, with the English clearly marked as translation. My article which appeared in 1990, still remains the only non-English-language paper in the literary journal.[4] Sadly, the journal is not published any more.

I have done this with a few other predominantly English journals. Sometimes when some newspapers have asked me to write a piece on a prominent personality that has departed, for instance, Chinua Achebe, Nelson Mandela or Nadine Gordimer, I have included a poem in Gĩkũyũ. And that is how some of my poems have found venues in English newspapers in Kenya, South Africa and elsewhere. Here, translation has helped me smuggle Gĩkũyũ poems into the English mainstream.

4 Ngũgĩ wa Thiong'o, 'Kĩĩngeretha: Rũthiomi rwa Thĩ Yoothe? Kaba gĩtwaĩri' / 'English: A Language for the World?', *Yale Journal of Criticism* 4(1) (1990): 269–93.

But there has been a more recent collaboration that was a conscious act from the inception to publication. I want to share this experience with you, today.

In February 2013, I went to Hawaii to be the keynote speaker at the University of Hawai'i's Words in the World symposium. I heard the Samoan writer Albert Wendt read from his book of poetry, *From Manoa to a Ponsonby Garden* (2012). I responded to his readings by an instant composition of a verse in Gĩkũyũ, 'Mũgũnda ũrĩa ũngĩ' [The Other Garden]. It was a kind of call and response, and it seemed to strike a chord in the conference attended by many delegates from America, the Pacific Islands and Asia. Certainly, it did so with the editors of the *Hawai'i Review,* who planned their 79th issue as a 'Call & Response'. They invited me to contribute the poem, which, by then, had expanded a lot.[5]

The verse which I prefer to call a chant is about my wife's garden at the back of our house on University Hills, UC–Irvine. The chant is informed by my world view articulated in my book *Globalectics,* which is essentially an expansion of the Blakean vision of seeing the world in a grain of sand, eternity in an hour. Based on that backyard, I am able to bring Kenya, California, Native America, Hawai'i, Samoa, Fiji and Aotearoa (New Zealand) into conversation.

My globalectic world view, that any centre can be the centre of the world, also informs my view of languages big and small.

5 Ngũgĩ wa Thiong'o, 'Mũgũnda ũrĩa ũngĩ' [The Other Garden], *Hawai'i Review* 79 (*Call & Response*) (2014): 10–45. Available at https://bit.ly/-3wreEX2 (last accessed on 14 June 2022).

This is because the globalectic world view looks at nature, society, thought, not as a hierarchy of power relations—the current and dominant view—but as a network of give-and-take. A network has no actual centre. It is what is expressed in a handshake, what in Gĩkũyũ is called *ngeithi*, a central image in the Gĩkũyũ poetic tradition called Gĩcandĩ. Seen in terms of network, there is no small or big language; they each give and receive.

I have argued elsewhere that translation is the common language of languages. But languages seen in terms of hierarchies of power and domination distort its full function as a common heritage of languages. As a network of relations of wealth, power and values, translation plays its crucial and ultimate role of enabling mutuality of being and becoming. In such a network, the voice of the translator will have the visibility it so much deserves. It becomes the voice of all languages.

Languages as Bridges

A bridge assumes an existing gulf, almost impassable ordinarily, between two entities. A bridge enables the crossings across the gulf. The nature of the gulf dictates the design and architecture of the bridge. Recognition and assessment of the gulf is essential in determining the necessary bridge. In other words, you do not spend resources and energy building bridges where there are no gulfs to cross.

A bridge enables a constant to-and-fro between two entities—in short, enables crossings, transitions and even continuities. In other words, a bridge is not a one-way crossing, for exodus only. This image therefore brings to the fore the intellectual and artistic wealth that could be an enormous commonwealth if we built bridges to enable crossings.

The opposite of a bridge is a wall, a barrier, that which bars contact and exchange—or if there is contact and exchange, it is that of the horse and the rider. For, remember that between the

---

Based on an address at the Garden City Literary Festival, Port Harcourt, Nigeria, 23–26 September 2009.

horse and the rider, there is plenty of contact, exchange, and even flow of trust and affection. But the structural basis of their relationship is that of a dictator and the dictated. Power relationship, even where it enables contact, can be a barrier to mutually beneficial crossings, transitions and continuities between languages and cultures.

Unfortunately, relationships between languages have not always been characterized by the image of the bridge but by that of the wall. This is the wall of the inequality of power. The inequality has basis in economics and politics, but philosophically, its roots lie in the conception of the relationship between languages in terms of hierarchy, a kind of linguistic feudalism and linguistic Darwinism.

Linguistic and cultural feudalism is the view consciously or unconsciously held that some languages, between and even within nations, are of a higher order than others; that they constitute an aristocracy while others, in a descending order of being, occupy lesser positions, different degrees of minionage.

This is because the dominant languages are perceived, even by the dominated, as having all the magic power of knowledge and production of ideas—culture itself—whereas the dominated languages are seen as having the opposite. They are incapable of producing knowledge, good ideas and good art.

The perception has nothing to do with the inherent powers of languages. It has been brought about by a historical process. In my book, *Decolonising the Mind* (1986), I told the story of my relationship to my mother tongue, Gĩkũyũ, and my language of education, English. English was also the official language of the colonial state. I wrote about how we used to be punished when we were caught speaking an African language in the school compound. We were humiliated by being made to carry a placard we called 'monitor' around our necks, literally stating that we were stupid. Thus, humiliation and negativity were attached to African languages in the learning process. A good performance in English on the other hand was greeted with acclaim. Two things were taking place in the cognitive process: positive affirmation of English as a means of intellectual production; and criminalization of African languages as means of knowledge production. With English, went pride; with African languages, shame. For a long time, I used to think that this was an African problem.

But some years ago, when I was researching my new book *Something Torn and New* (2009), I found out that what was done to Africans had already been done to the Welsh. In nineteenth century, Welsh kids caught speaking their mother tongue in the school compound were also humiliated by being made to carry a sign around their necks that read 'WN / Welsh Not'. At the very least, my colonial story had been re-enacted in Wales.

A question frequently asked, after I talk about the necessity of using African languages as literary instruments, is that of the multiplicity of languages. But many languages within nations can be a strength if the relationship between them is not based on notions of hierarchy but on those of a network.

In the vision of a network, there is not one centre; there are several centres equidistant from one another but connected in a give-and-take relationship. Every language draws from another. Every language gives to another. All languages end up giving to and taking from each other, laying the groundwork for a complex independence and interdependence within and between cultures.

But how do they do that? Or, rather, how would they do that? By building bridges between them, through translations. Translation is what enables that traffic of ideas between languages. In his book *Discourse on Colonialism* (2000), the Martinican poet Aimé Césaire described cultural contact and exchange as the oxygen of civilization. Language networking through translation can only help in the generation of that oxygen within and between nations.

The translator is the maker of bridges between languages. Translations have played an important role in the history of ideas. The much-talked-about European Renaissance would have been impossible without translations. Christianity and Islam and their spread all over the world have been enormously aided by the translations of the Bible and the Koran. Translations and translators can play an even bigger role in the African renaissance. In *Something Torn and New*, I have talked of translations between African languages; translations from europhone African literature into African languages; the translations of diasporic works of Caribbean and African American writers into African languages in a vision I describe as 'Restoration'; and finally, the translations of the finest traditions in world cultures into African languages. This bridge building would have a big impact in the restoration of pride, initiatives and productivity to Africa.

Preface to the Kurdish Translation of *Decolonising the Mind*

The lectures that became the book *Decolonising the Mind* were first given at the University of Auckland, New Zealand, in 1984 under the title 'The Politics of Language in African Literature'. The hall was always crowded with students and faculty at first, but towards the end the lectures attracted Māori and other Pacific communities from outside the university and the city. After the last lecture, a young Māori lady offered me a painted gourd. 'You were not talking about Africa, you were talking about us—Māori people in New Zealand.' They too had been fighting for the survival and revival of their language from English domination. Since its publication in 1986, the book has elicited similar reactions in many parts of the world. This just confirms that the issues raised in *Decolonising the Mind* are pertinent to the experiences, histories and cultures wherever in the world people have been subjugated by others.

In all such cases, the subjugators have always imposed their language on the subjugated. This is because, for its success and effectiveness, a system of economic and political domination is dependent on cultural and psychological control. If we think of culture as the eyes through which a people see the world, the implications of a people being denied their language and having to use the language of the dominating power become clear. The aim and the result are to make the dominated people look at themselves and their place in the world through the eyes of the dominant social forces. That's why language control has always been at the centre of imperial cultural and psychological conquests.

Imperial enterprises, conquests and control have made the world embrace the relations between languages in terms of hierarchies of power. The languages of conquest see themselves as inherently more of languages than other languages. They try and make the subjugated view the language of conquest as the one with knowledge, information and beauty. The language of conquest becomes the language of being. A people so subjected may even come to see their own language as that of non-being.

Therefore, for such peoples, language emancipation is a necessary component of psychological emancipation. For, in reality there is no language which is inherently more of a language than any other language; all languages, big and small, are equal in their potentialities. I would like to see a global rejection of language relations in terms of hierarchy, and a global embrace of the relationship in terms of a network. In a network situation, there are no big or small languages, because all languages, within a country, or across countries and nations, will relate on the basis of equal give-and-take. Languages that help inter-language communications will just be that: help language dialogue and not language death.

If you know all the languages of the world and you don't know your mother tongue or the language of your culture, that is enslavement. But if you know your mother tongue or the language of your culture, and add all other languages to it, that is empowerment.

In reality it is impossible for any person to know all the languages in their own country, let alone in the world. This is where the art of translation comes in. Translation makes dialogue between languages and cultures and different histories easier and more enriching. I would like to see translation elevated to centre stage in relations between languages and cultures.

It is in that context that I really welcome this translation of *Decolonising the Mind* into Kurdish. I hope the readers will find some of the ideas relevant to their own histories, struggles and experiences. Linguistic emancipation anywhere is central to the emancipation of the mind everywhere.

An Archipelago of Treasures

I want to express hearty appreciations and offer congratulations to Archipelago Books for what they have already done and accomplished. *Feliz decimo aniversario*!

When recently two of my children, Mũkoma wa Ngũgĩ, and Wanjikũ wa Ngũgĩ, had the German translations of their books, *Nairobi Heat* and *The Fall of Saints*, released, we looked at one another, through Skype, and said: they look like real books. We could not read German, but we had the consolation, from how the way the editions looked or the feel of the paper, that they did indeed look like real books. This, I must say, was in comparison and contrast not only to how their English versions looked but also to the electronic and PDF versions of books in general. With virtual reality, books no longer look like books.

But if there is just one thing that one can say about Archipelago, it is that all the books that they produce look like

---

Talk given at the Archipelago Books' Tenth Anniversary Gala at Wythe Hotel, Brooklyn, 16 October 2014.

real books all the time. Each of their products, for the last ten years, are a pleasure to look, hold and touch.

I am mindful of the proverb that warns us no to judge a book by its cover, but in the case of Archipelago, the content of the book matches the form of its appearance. Different readers may differ over that judgement, and it is okay, for tastes differ even over the best-prepared dish. But there is one aspect of what Archipelago produces that is not subject to different tastes or interpretations. The number of languages from which they have drawn is amazing—at least twenty-one different languages, if I am not mistaken. By so doing they have brought many languages and cultures, from the Icelandic, Chinese, Croatian, Catalonian and Bengali to the French, Arabic and German, into conversation, albeit in English.

They have done this through the one language common to all languages, no, not English, but rather the one we call Translation. For if there is one language that all languages speak, its name is Translation. Translation is the language of all languages, and Archipelago Books has used it to the enrichment of all our lives, without, dare I say, uprooting the writers from their different cultures and languages.

I emphasize this because, many writers in the world, particularly from Africa and Asia, have become captives of the metaphysical empires of the dominant European languages. Their product, europhonism, has uprooted many writers and intellectuals from their languages: it has made many have the illusion that they can only meaningfully dream and imagine in French and English.

Even when they draw from their languages, it is as antiques drawn from archaeological sites to decorate their English and French quarters. For them, African and other indigenous languages are a lower rung in the ladder to an English heaven. Or rather, they think that heaven is divided into French, German, Spanish and English zones, and the quickest and straightest ways are European linguistic ladders.

It is not just the writers. The entire publishing and book distribution industry largely behaves and acts as if the destiny of the world is a European heaven. The keys the angels hold at the gates of heaven are made in Paris, London or New York.

By emphasizing translations, thus acknowledging that all languages, big and small, carry precious and unique treasures of the mind, Archipelago Books are laying and emphasizing the real foundation for what Johan Wolfgang Goethe once called world literature, a term which is back in literary and academic circulation. Goethe of course saw that literature, not in one or two national languages but in different ones that then dialogued with one another through translations.

But looking at the Archipelago list, the statistics tell us that their work is only beginning. Of the twenty-one languages that I was able to count from their current catalogue, sixteen were European, six from the rest of the world. African languages don't figure at all. I know that in their journal *Imagine Africa* there have been translations from Gĩkũyũ and Yoruba, at least. This is no small gesture but more could be done. I would like to see more book-length translations from African languages, and hopefully also into African languages. Even within the linguistic boundaries already set by the location of the publishing house, still more can be done to bring the treasures in African and other indigenous languages into conversation with others through the universal language of translation.

An important development in the case of production in African languages is about to occur. A wealthy African philanthropist in Kenya has given Cornell University funds for the Mabati-Cornell Kiswahili Prize for African Literature, that offers an annual prize of 10,000 US dollars for the winning Kiswahili language novel.[1] This is huge. Up to now, prizes have been given to Africans on the condition that they don't write in an African language. Not writing in an African language has become the condition set by the prize donors to African writing! What an insult to the largest continent in the world!

I very much hope that the Archipelago Books will work with the Mabati-Cornell Prize and similar efforts that may spring from this, so that translations will be available without uprooting the writers from African languages. The last ten years have been an incredible beginning. I really look forward to what Archipelago Books produces in the next ten years: help turn all the languages of the earth into a united archipelago of boundless and shared treasures.

---

1 Now called 'The Safal-Cornell Kiswahili Prize for African Literature'. Available at: https://kiswahiliprize.cornell.edu/ (last accessed: 14 June 2022).

Adventures in Translation

I wrote *Caitaani Mũtharabainĩ* [*Devil on the Cross*], in a maximum-security prison. It was my first novel in the Gĩkũyũ language. And I wrote it in my mother tongue because I'd been put in prison because of a play, *I Will Marry When I Want,* or *Ngaahika Ndeenda,* which I had written with Ngũgĩ wa Mĩriĩ in the Gĩkũyũ. See the irony? Put in prison by an African government, for writing in an African language. In prison, I thought about the issue of language and I decided that my novels and my creative work from then onwards would be in the language which was the basis of my incarceration. When I came out of prison in 1978, Henry Chakava of Heinemann Kenya made an offer. A month or so before publication, the publisher started getting death threats. And a week before he was due to release it, some 'thugs' accosted him at the gates of his house in Nairobi and, as he got out of his car, they grabbed him and tried to push him into the boot of their own. Fortunately, another vehicle happened to

---

This essay has been adapted from the Writers' Centre Norwich lecture given on 20 January 2017 at Goldsmiths, University of London.

pass by and foiled the kidnapping attempt. So instead, they cut off his finger with a machete. Henry Chakava still went ahead and brought out the Gĩkũyũ original of *Devil on the Cross*.

The second adventure was after my being forced into exile in London, in 1982. I wrote the novel *Matigari*, or *Matigari ma Njirungi* in Gĩkũyũ, almost in defiance to my exile in a totally English-speaking environment. Again Chakava published it, in 1986. In Kenya people started talking about the main character, Matigari, a survivor of the liberation war who went around the country asking searching questions about truth and justice. The intelligence services of the Daniel arap Moi dictatorship reported that this guy called Matigari was defying orders about 'rumour mongering'. It was illegal in Kenya then to 'rumour monger', so they sent police officers to arrest him only to find that he was a character in fiction. Instead, they literally arrested the book. In a coordinated operation, they went to all the bookshops at the same time, pretending to be booksellers from another town, who had sold out all their copies because of high demand. Once the bookseller showed them the stock, the would-be book buyers showed their police badges and confiscated all the copies. So there's a time when the novel wasn't available anywhere in Kenya. For some years *Matigari* lived abroad, exiled in an English translation by Wangui wa Goro.

My third novel in the Gĩkũyũ language was *Mũrogi wa Kagogo* [*Wizard of the Crow*]. I wrote it in exile in California. My wife Njeeri and I returned to Kenya in 2003 to launch the Gĩkũyũ-language publication of the novel before the English version had come out. So we got to Kenya, and eleven days before the publication of the novel, armed gunmen burst into our hotel room, and we barely escaped with our lives. By the way, the English translation, *Wizard of the Crow,* won the 2006 California Book Award Gold Medal, an award once won by John Steinbeck for *The Grapes of Wrath*. Now, I'm only narrating this to show the impact—the fear or the terror or the whatever-you-want-to-call-it—that the publication of my works in Gĩkũyũ has generated. The first work in Gĩkũyũ proper was actually the play *I Will Marry When I Want*. That sent me to a maximum-security prison. For the second, *Devil on the Cross*, the publisher lost his finger. With the third, the hero is almost arrested except for the fact he is fictional. On the occasion of the fourth one, my wife and I nearly lost our lives. So these 'unreadable' works must be saying something or demonstrating something, which an oppressive regime understood very clearly and which Adewale, perceptive as he is in so many ways, could not quite see. These works in Gĩkũyũ narrate my life in writing and translation, and it continues to this day, but with a positive outcome. And this is the story I want to share with you. Another adventure in translation.

In 2008, I asked my then thirteen-year-old son Thiong'o to write me some short fiction as a kind of seasonal gift—a combination of Christmas, Kwanzaa and the New Year. He delivered his first-ever short story, *Henry and I*, a Christmas story; and the following year he turned the tables on me. A day before Christmas he demanded a story from me. I delivered *Song of a Bee,* now published as a book by East African Educational Publishers but only in the Gĩkũyũ language. It has become a tradition in our house in Southern California: for birthdays and seasons we sometimes exchange stories instead of material gifts. It's not always easy, especially for me, for they nearly always wait until the day before to make demands on me—it's a kind of challenge. 'Tomorrow's my birthday, and for my gift I want a story from you.' I remember once Mũmbi, who is Thiong'o's older sister by a year, asked for a story for her birthday present, again really at the last minute. By then she was already a college student. And this time I really had writer's block. I turned over many ideas in my head, until I recalled her fascination with dialectics. She was studying philosophy at the time, from Plato to Hegel. She was especially intrigued by the number *one*, which arose from her work on Plotinus (who took the one ultimate reality of Philo of Alexandria for whom one was God's number, the basis of all the other numbers), and in our daily conversations she would go over and over the idea of the one containing many, and being contained in the many in different variations. This is where I got the idea for what became *Ituĩka Rĩa Mũrũngarũ: Kana Kĩrĩa Gĩtũmaga Andũ Mathiĩ Marũngiĩ* [*The Upright Revolution, or Why Humans Walk Upright*]. I drew on the workings of the human body, which, after all, is our primary field of knowledge.

The story tells of the epic struggle between legs and hands for dominance of the human body. You see, the two limbs are so similar that they had to have gone through a phase of sibling rivalry, which in this case ends with a tournament attended by all nature to settle once and for all who are the more important to the body:

hands or legs (at the time of this epic struggle humans walked on all fours like any other four-legged creatures). The story makes a few jibes about Mouth who talks of 'my this my that' as if it owned every other organ—and of course, many presidents and kings and priests tend to talk all 'my this my that, I'll do this and that,' forgetting the concept and the reality of 'we'. When the 'I' replaces the 'we', we are in trouble, as the contending and quarrelling pair of limbs soon find out. So in one sense it's the story of the critic's tendency to explain the complexities of any whole through the one-sidedness of class, race, ethnicity and religion. But in the end *The Upright Revolution* is just a fable, and my daughter enjoyed it as a story and not as a treatise on politics and philosophy.

I thought no more about the story until a year later when my other son, Mũkoma wa Ngũgĩ, author of *Nairobi Heat* (2011) and currently a professor of English at Cornell University, told me that he had been approached by Moses Kilolo, on behalf of a group of young people in Kenya who called themselves a pan-African writers' collective, to ask me if I could write a story in Gĩkũyũ for their journal, *Jalada*, which was going to release an issue on translation. I thought Mũkoma was playing games with me. Young people wanting a story in an African language!

Ever since I wrote my book *Decolonising the Mind* back in 1984, calling on African intellectuals to start producing ideas in African languages instead of English, French and Portuguese, I have faced everything from hostility to polite applause at the possibility—but no real change in practice. I've even seen African and international organizations give prizes to promote African literature on the condition that Africans don't do it in an African language. Submissions must be in a European language only. And yet the prizes are there to promote African literature and African writers. When you come to think of it, the assumption that Africans can only can be African by the grace of European tongues is actually quite offensive. It's as if all of those people who built the Egyptian pyramids, the marvellous city civilizations along the East African coast, or the great Ethiopian cathedrals, spoke English, French or Portuguese. In Kenya, some students and teachers admonish those who speak English with an accent affected by their African languages of birth with a derogatory term: 'shrubbing'. The word comes from the noun 'shrub', and shrub from 'bush'. The 'bush' as an image of Africa has a long history going all the way back to colonial times, and now an African elite is using it against Africa. And these will be the policy makers of tomorrow. I've often spoken about how Europe gave Africa the resources of her accents in exchange for Africa giving Europe access to the resources of a continent. That explains why a continent bigger than North America, Europe, China and India put together, a continent endowed with more natural resources than any other, continues to lag behind in terms of development. Accents for access is really the story of modern Africa.

So you can understand my shock at the request from the *Jalada* pan-African writers' collective for a story in an African language. Put yourself in my shoes or in my head, and you can imagine my reaction to the request: this is my chance to write the most perfect story I can, the best story in the world if possible.

But unfortunately, my mouth suddenly dried up. I have never been so frustrated with my inability to write something new. My experience of writing stories on demand was not much of a help. It was then that I remembered the fable that I had written for Mũmbi as a gift. I sent it to Mũkoma, who sent it to Kilolo, editor-in-chief of the magazine. I could hardly believe it when, early in 2016, he told me that within a year of its publication *The Upright Revolution* had been translated into more than fifty-four languages in the world, forty of them African, along with six European, six Asian and two Middle Eastern (Arabic and Kurdish). It was published in an Indian-language newspaper with a readership, according to the editor, of two million. And later that year, Modernista publishers in Sweden released the Swedish translation of the story as a small book. The drama of the translation has generated news. The *Guardian* gave it a full page,[1] and then it was on social media, and many people came to know about the story through that and through the editors of the *New York Times* tweeting about it. These translations have raised a debate as to whether *The Upright Revolution* is the most translated story in the world. I'm sure there must be others, of course, that are more translated, but I think I can certainly say it is probably the most translated story in Africa.

Now, I want to make clear that the story was just one of many items buried in my hard drive. And so it could have remained, like many others I wrote in Gĩkũyũ, since publishers

1 Alison Flood, 'Short Story by Ngũgĩ wa Thiong'o Translated into over 30 languages in One Publication', *Guardian*, 29 March 2016.

are still slow-footed when it comes to publishing books in African languages. This one would have met the same fate had not Kilolo and his group called it back to life. And that's why I describe this group, the *Jalada* pan-African writers' collective, as practical visionaries—because they put the theory of translation into collective practice. And we need more of this. Put it this way: when Wangui wa Goro translated *Matigari*, she was one. Now there are many doing the same. So, whatever the ultimate destiny of their translation projects, their success with *The Upright Revolution* has challenged in a very practical way existing orthodoxies about African languages and their relationships with one another.

I have argued about these orthodoxies in *Decolonising the Mind*, a text which has become central in the emerging decolonialist ideas and aesthetics and the calls for the decolonization of institutions of higher learning. When I first published the book, I had thought that the language question and the need for decolonization were confined to Africa's relationship to Europe. Since then I've come to see that it is a global problem: whenever one people has conquered another, they have always imposed their language on the subjugated. The English did it to the Irish; I might also add, to the Scots and the Welsh. The Japanese, during the colonial occupation of Korea (1910–1945) did the same thing—imposed the Japanese language and names on the Koreans. Native Americans, as well as natives of Canada, New Zealand and Australia, similarly lost out to the dominant English or Spanish. Hawaiians lost their language when they were incorporated into the United States of America; it was actually banned and only restored in 1978. Even in Europe, Sámi people in Norway found their language subjugated in the same way as other languages in America and Africa. Today the Sámi language is protected and even supported by the Norwegian state but that was not always the case. They were forced to abandon their language and to take on, to internalize, Norwegian.

The struggle for power between languages is always part of a much bigger problem that holds back the development of global humanity. This bigger problem lies in the conception of society and cultures in terms of hierarchy. And that conception is itself a product of what I like to think of as imperial reason: the drive to conquer and master. For imperial reason, hierarchy is the essence of being. It was the logic behind colonialism and now globalization, for both are built on the philosophy and structure of the few over the many. Imperialism dictates that in order for a few countries to thrive, they must deprive the many countries of their resources. And within countries, that in order for there to be a few millionaires, millions must be poor. In order for a few to be healthy, many must be diseased. In the world today the gap of wealth and power between a handful of wealthy nations and the majority of poor nations is deepening and widening, and the wealth of the few is dependent on gobbling up 90 per cent of the resources of poorer nations.[2]

---

2 Jason Hickel, 'Aid in Reverse: How Poor Countries Develop Rich Countries', *Guardian*, 14 January 2017. Available at: https://bit.ly/3frE5T3 (last accessed on 20 June 2022).

Imperial reason is seen in the freedom of financial capital to move in and out of nations without barriers, followed shortly thereafter by the erection of barriers and even physical walls against the movement of labour that follows the destiny of the stolen resources. And within nations the gap of wealth and power between a minority of haves and a majority of have-nots is also deepening and widening. Wealth and power are dependent on the resources of the many, yet recent studies indicate that the world's nine richest men (they are mostly men) control more resources than two-thirds of the world's population.[3] Nine people possess more wealth than half the planet combined. The result is the splendour of a few and the squalor of the many; the number of prisoners, beggars and the homeless are growing rapidly in many nations. So when you walk in a city of any developed nation, you are likely to encounter the beggar and the homeless at the door or in the streets. Interestingly, the prisoner is hidden away—although some countries have more than two million people incarcerated and support privately owned prison industries with billionaires at the top. It sounds like fiction, but America has more than two million people in prison.[4] The population of Iceland is a little above quarter million. So, if 2.3 million people

3 Sarah Jacobs, 'Just Nine of the World's Richest Men Have More Combined Wealth than the Poorest 4 Billion People', *Independent*, 17 January 2018. Available at: https://bit.ly/3Dn7oOH (last accessed on 20 June 2022).

4 Peter Wagner and Wanda Bertram, 'What Percent of the US Is Incarcerated? (And Other Ways to Measure Mass incarceration)', *Prison Policy Initiative*, 16 January 2020. Available at: https://bit.ly/3WgkZ2U (last accessed on 20 June 2022).

are incarcerated, it's like having six or seven Icelandic nations in prison, correct? But we don't see them because they are hidden. America is not alone—this happens all over the world: the prison population is increasing but hidden and therefore invisible, as if it doesn't exist.

Hierarchy as a conception of being is more clearly reflected in the relationship between languages. What's wrong with the world or even within one country is not the existence of many languages and cultures but, rather, their relating to each other based on the notion that one language is inherently better than other, or even that for one language to be, others must cease to be. Even a national language, desirable as it may be for purposes of communication across different communities, is often built on the graveyard of other languages.

Now, all languages in the world, big and small, have a lot to contribute to the enrichment of our common human culture. We already see this in the way we enjoy the literature and music of different languages and cultures. And each language has its unique musicality. So relations between languages and cultures are a good thing. But that contact cannot be that of the rider and the horse. Languages and cultures can and should relate in terms of network, not hierarchy. And a network is really a system of give-and-take between equals. Translation is central to this entire system. It cannot be overstated that translation has played a great role in human history. But translation can only achieve the role of enabling conversation if it's based on an assumption of equality among participating languages. So if you ask me about the importance of the *Jalada* translation project and the success of their press, yes: the success of having *The Upright Revolution* translated into 61 languages points to a resolution of what has often been viewed as a problem in the creation of modern nations in Africa. Any work written in any one of the several languages within a contemporary African nation can be translated into all the other languages within the same nation. (In a way, the Bible is a good example of this. The content of the Bible is the same, and through the grace and power of translations, all those who call themselves Christians share the same content, although they access it through translation, reading the content in their respective languages.) Equally importantly, the project helps to negate the colonially inherited assumptions that African languages are not capable of intellectual production. *The Upright Revolution*, though originally written in Gĩkũyũ, is now available to many communities in Africa and beyond which can now read the dialectics of the human body in their own languages. So I'd like to end by rephrasing Aimé Césaire's maxim that cultural contact is the oxygen of civilization with a statement to the effect that language contact through translation is the real oxygen of civilization. And in a small way, the *Jalada* translation initiative has proven this truth and shown the way for the future.

The Politics of Translation

Notes towards an African Language Policy

Recently I published a collection of essays with Seagull Books, under the title *Secure the Base: Making Africa Visible in the World* (2016). When two armies fight, they protect their respective bases while trying to destabilize and even capture their opponent's. Both sides gather intelligence about the other's base through covert and overt means. But suppose the spies sent to the other side are held captives or willingly enjoy the reception, so that instead of sending back what they know, they give away the information about their own base? One side is said to lose a battle when their base is overrun by enemy forces. If the defeated want to fight back, they try

This paper was presented as the Neville Alexander Memorial Lecture at the Harvard University Center for African Studies, Cambridge, Massachusetts, on 19 April 2016. I want to thank the center and the Harvard University Department of African and African American Studies for inviting me and my wife Njeeri, and to congratulate John Mũgane and the African Languages Program for the tremendous work they have done and continue to do with and for African languages.

and secure their base. The security of one's base, even when two armies are cooperating to achieve a jointly held tactical or strategic end against a third, is necessary. So either in opposition or in cooperation, fighting units keep their bases secure and not in disarray.

In the history of conquest, the first thing the victorious conqueror does is attack people's names and languages. The idea is to deny them the authority of naming the self and the world, to delegitimize the history and the knowledge they already possess, delegitimize their own language as a credible source of knowledge and definition of the world, so that the conqueror's language can become the source of the very definition of being. This was true with the English conquest of Ireland, Wales, Scotland, or the Japanese conquest of South Korea; or the USA's takeover of Hawaii: ban or weaken the languages of the conquered, then impose by gun, guise or guile their own language and accord it all the authority of naming the world. It was done with the enslaved. African languages and names were banned in the plantations; and later in the continent as a whole—so much so that that African people now accept europhony to define their countries and who they are: francophone, anglophone or lusophone.

I invite you to keep in mind the image of the base and the relationships between bases—hostile or hospitable—as I offer some notes towards an African language policy and the role of inter-African-languages translation in that process.

Neville Alexander, whom we have come to honour with this annual lecture, was a noble warrior for multilingualism and the driving force behind the 11-language policy of post-apartheid South Africa. The language struggles between English and Afrikaans, and between both and African languages, had always been part of the country's history and it reflected the underlying struggles for economic and political power and dominance among the racial communities. Similar struggles between European and African languages prevail in all the other African countries. But South Africa is one of the few that have not shied away from the challenge of formulating a policy which recognizes multilingualism as the founding social reality of the nation. The consistent and effective implementation of the policy is another matter, but its very existence is important.

Some of course may want to argue that it is easier to do so as South Africa has only 11 languages to contend with, but what about other African countries where they have many more—hundreds even? But hundreds of languages also mean there are hundreds of communities that use them, and these communities constitute the geographic nation! This linguistic picture confronts policy makers as a nightmare; and they think that if they can ignore the nightmare long enough, or frighten it away with greater emphasis on European languages, the nightmare will vanish, and they will wake up to the bliss of a harmonious European-language-speaking African nation. So they engineer a massive transfer of resources from African to European languages. Ninety per cent of the resources earmarked for language education goes to European ones, a minuscule percentage to African languages, if at all. But reality, however, is stubborn, and policy makers wake up to the same nightmare. European-language speakers in any one of the African nations is at most 10 per cent of the population; the other 90 are speakers of African languages.

Ironically, in some countries, the colonial period had a more progressive language policy, which ensured basic literacy in the mother tongue. That was how I came to learn Gĩkũyũ. But at Independence, the four years' elementary education in mother tongue was scrapped. Through and by every means possible, children were immersed in English from kindergarten onwards. This resulted in a generation of Kenyans who could barely speak their mother tongue; or even if they spoke it, they could not read or write it. Belatedly, the state tried to rectify the damage and introduced mother tongue as a subject and even produced some texts to meet the need; but even these half-hearted efforts were later abandoned. In most schools, the hour earmarked for mother tongue is used for further drilling in English. The delegitimization of African languages as credible sources and basis of knowledge began in the colonial era and was completed and normalized in the postcolonial one.

Where English was now equated with the gate to progress and modernity, African languages came to be seen as barriers to that glittering thing. In Kenya, whenever and wherever a speaker's mother tongue made the speaker not able to pronounce certain English sounds, he was denounced as 'shrubbing' English. He had brought bush and darkness to obscure the light and clarity of English. In an article he published in *Jalada*, Mũkoma wa Ngũgĩ tells hilarious stories of African students in Kenya laughing outright at one another for 'shrubbing' English.[1] At a party in New Jersey some years ago, I was witness to a video that was supposedly very funny, of a Cabinet Minister who had difficulties in pronouncing long words like 'prosperity' and 'procrastination'. Before his appointment to the Cabinet, the minister had already proven himself as one of the most successful businessmen in the country, employing hundreds of university graduates. Yet in the video he is portrayed as ignorant and an object of fun and scorn.

Clearly, this view of African languages as synonymous with the darkness of the bush becomes a big barrier to imagining and therefore crafting a practical language policy. Another barrier is the fundamentalism of monolingualism. A nation is not really a nation without a common language to go with the commonality of territory, economy and culture. In this context, African languages, because of their huge numbers, are seen as anti-nationhood. Monolingualism is seen as the centripetal answer to the centrifugal anarchy of multiplicity of languages. European languages are seen as coming to the rescue of a cohesive Africa, otherwise threatened by its own languages. It is in the same vein as what colonial military expeditions touted as the pacification of primitive tribes; only now, in the postcolonial era, it is linguistic pacification of languages of anarchy and blood. The difference is that now it is the *African* governments and policy makers who are at the head of the linguistic pacification programmes. In the colonial

1 Mũkoma wa Ngũgĩ, 'Writing in African Languages: A Question for Our Times', *Jalada*, 15 September 2015. Available at: https://bit.ly/3wuc5DI (last accessed on 15 June 2022).

era, the slogan behind the pacification was ending tribal wars—Hobbes's war of all against all in a state of nature; now in the postcolonial era, it is ending ethnic wars fuelled by African languages. The subtext is that African languages are inherently incapable of relating to one another, but ironically they each can relate to English; especially when anglophone writing dives into them for a proverb or two to spice their literary offering to a europhone modernity of monolingualism.

In reality, there are very few, if any, monolingual nations in the world. What most have is an officially imposed language as the national language: the language of power. The language of power is a dictatorship of the monolingual on a plurality of languages and it negates the human right to one's language.

For Africa, and generally the postcolonial state, this dictatorship was first imposed by imperial powers, who put their language at the centre of the universe, the source of light. The postcolonial state merely nationalized the already linguistic dictatorship, which in effect means foreign languages assuming the mantle of the identity of the national. In reality, it is simply the borrowed language of the 10 per cent but spread across the nation. This acquired national language has the double character of being both foreign and elitist. And yet this is what is touted as its advantage: that it is equally accessible to the 10 per cent of each linguistic community and equally inaccessible to all the constituent communities. So its accessibility to the elite but its inaccessibility to the majority is therefore what makes it the best language to unify the country. The European-language-speaking elite thus sees itself as constituting the nation. European languages become the knight on a horse rescuing the postcolonial state, otherwise trapped within the linguistic House of Babel, by enabling communication across a problematic plurality.

The third barrier arises from fears of being left out of the heaven promised by globalization. This arises from the earlier colonially rooted notion that African languages are not modern enough and that European ones are the only ladder to the global heaven. If Africa promotes its languages, the continent will miss the train to heaven. But globalization is a function of finance capital, its dominance in the world, a logical development of historical capitalism from its mercantile phase, through its industrial, to its present phase where, as finance capital, and aided by technology, it smashes all state barriers to its movement. There must not be any barriers to movement of capital across state borders but there have to be barriers, even actual physical walls, to prevent the movement of labour across state barriers in pursuit of what that finance capital has stolen from their regions. The result, as I have stated elsewhere in my book *Secure the Base,* are states too weak to interfere with the operation of finance capital but strong enough to police the population, should they dare to do something about it and its negative impact on their lives. For example, in the postcolonial state, the police and the military have been used many more times against the population than against any external threat. The joint military exercises that the Western powers have with the militaries of postcolonial states have never been for purposes of a jointly perceived threat from a third country; otherwise they would also be having joint military exercises on the soil of France, Britain and America.

But, for some reason, globalization—despite the control of resources by Western corporate capital—is seen as a good thing and African languages seem to stand in the way of the elite receiving their share of 'global goodies'. In *Secure the Base*, I have tried to make the distinction between and globalism and globalization. Globalization is really 'gobblization' of other people's resources by a greedy corporate elite protected by the might of imperial powers. Globalism is a form of social networking of peoples across race, regions and religions, and it tries to mobilize people against corporate greed and its divisive tactics.

The fourth barrier to a comprehensive and all-embracing national policy is the conception of the relationship of languages in terms of hierarchy, with the officially sanctioned language sitting at the top, as the language of power, law, justice, education, administration and economic exchange. If that language is the former colonial language and officials want to replace it, they can only think of choosing one African language among the many to occupy the same position in the hierarchy. The prospect of 'the one' becoming the new language of power rings alarm bells in the speakers of other languages.

Hierarchy is not inherent in plurality. The plural can relate either vertically as in steps of a ladder—a hierarchical relation—or horizontally as when people link arms to form a line or a circle—a network. Both are relational but the hierarchical one means the energy of the higher suffocating the lower, while the network means shared synergy from the contact.

Together, the four barriers (I am sure there are others) form a kind of orthodoxy, with the assumptions behind it normalized as self-evident truth. Orthodoxy becomes an invisible boulder that cannot be moved; the very thought of moving it tires the mind. The prospects of hopelessness prevent us from even making a gesture.

Border communities challenge that orthodoxy. Communities that exist on either side of national boundaries speak a variety of languages, but the relationship between the languages is not hierarchical but, rather, 'networkly'. Hierarchy is a question of power. It assumes that some languages are more of a language than other languages. But the notion of a network assumes a give-and-take: and that there is no language which is more of a language than another language.

Of course, border communities do face the challenge of a member of one language group being able to communicate with the member of another. They solve this through multilingualism: most are polyglots. But in addition to that, sometimes there develops a lingua franca among them, but this lingua franca functions differently from the language of power. A language of power assumes that for it to be, other languages must cease. It desires to replace or silence all the other languages. But a lingua franca assumes the existence of co-equal languages. It simply facilitates communication and dialogue among language equals. The condition of the existence of one is the existence of all. The lingua franca helps the give-and-take of a network of languages. It does not replace them. Such a lingua franca is often a distinctive language but known by most other language speakers in addition to their own.

Translation—a kind of dialogue or conversation among languages—is another challenge to the orthodoxy. The *Jalada* translation project, an instance of that challenge, is unfolding before our very eyes. *Jalada* is an online literary journal run by a pan-African collective, a group of young people who come from different parts of the continent.[2] *Jalada*'s editor-in-chief Moses Kilolo comes from Kenya. *Jalada* is a journal in English but, ironically, what has created the waves is not their English writings but their translation project. In a recent article, Mũkoma wa Ngũgi described the effort as 'a revolution in many tongues'.[3] This was very strong praise for their first and, so far, only translation issue. I feel honoured that this first translation issue features my own story, *Ituĩka rĩa Mũrũngarũ: Kana Kĩrĩa Gĩtũmaga Andũ Mathiĩ Marũngiĩ*, written in Gĩkũyũ, later translated as *The Upright Revolution: Or, Why Humans Walk Upright.*

The story was translated into more than thirty African languages—the most translated story on the continent, according to the *Guardian*, which carried the news analysis of the phenomenon. It is indeed rare for the publication of a story to become

2 Available at: https://jaladaafrica.org/ (last accessed: 15 June 2022).

3 Mũkoma wa Ngũgi, 'A Revolution in Many Tongues', *Africa Is a Country*, 4 August 2016. Available at: https://bit.ly/3FvZUvi (last accessed on 13 June 2022).

news, but several newspapers carried reports on the *Jalada* translation feat. Recently, a Sunday magazine from Bangalore, India, carried a Kannada translation for their three million readers. Three million readers for a story originating in an African language—that in itself is another story. Translations into more languages in and outside Africa continue, and *Jalada* is hoping to release another issue with the new batch of translations.

Translations as such are not a new phenomenon in Africa. Of the evening stories that left a mark on me as a child was one about a father, his son and their donkey, who, trying to live up to every opinion of neighbours and strangers as to who should carry whom, end up carrying the donkey on their shoulders. Later, when I learnt to read and write, I was very surprised to come across the same story, but with the added pleasure of illustrations. The image of a donkey hanging upside down from a pole supported by the shoulders of father and son, with the market crowd laughing at their foolishness, still lives within me.

The storyteller in the evening must have oralized the story from its literary source, a process that I have described in my book *Globalectics: Theory and Politics of Knowing*. It is only last year in Irvine, seventy years after my childhood encounter with it, that I made another discovery, thanks to my YouTube lessons in Spanish. The story was a free translation and adaptation of the Spanish story '¿Padre hijo o caballo?' by the medieval Spanish writer Don Juan Manuel. Only that in the Gĩkũyũ-language version the horse becomes the donkey. Whatever the sequence, the story, through translation, was now part of my Gĩkũyũ culture.

The Bible in Gĩkũyũ, another part of my culture, was a translation of a series of translations, English, Latin, Greek, Hebrew, and Aramaic all the way back to whatever language that God, Adam and Eve used in the Garden of Eden. I was very impressed by the fact that Jesus and all the characters in the New and Old Testament spoke Gĩkũyũ! Even God, in the Garden of Eden, spoke Gĩkũyũ!

This inheritance from translation is not unique to Gĩkũyũ or to Africa. The Bible in translation has similarly had an impact on the growth of many languages in the world. In my memoir, *In the House of the Interpreter,* I have talked of my Scottish teacher who used to say that Jesus spoke very simple English. Not just the Bible! The translation of the Greek and Latin classics into English, French and German not only aided in the growth of the languages but the same classics, in their translation, have made an impact on the study and development of drama, poetry and philosophy in general. It is impossible to imagine Shakespeare without translations. He worked within a culture where translations from other languages into the emerging national tongues were the literary equivalent of piracy for silver and gold on the high seas, a phenomenon I first mentioned in my book on the politics of memory, titled *Something Torn and New: Towards an African Renaissance.*

The *Jalada* translation project then has clearly followed on one of the most consistent threads in world cultures, but similar translation trends can be seen in Africa. The East Africa Educational Publishers have brought out Kiswahili translations of most of the classics of African fiction originally written in English,

French and Portuguese. In his article 'Revolution in Many Tongues', Mũkoma wa Ngũgĩ has detailed other efforts in this direction, citing, for instance, Boubacar Boris Diop of Senegal, who has set up a publishing outfit, Ceytu, dedicated to publishing Wolof translations of major classics of African thought, such as Frantz Fanon's *The Wretched of the Earth*. In 2014 SUNY Press bought out a book titled *Listening to Ourselves: A Multilingual Anthology of African Philosophy*. Compiled and edited by the African-Caribbean-Canadian intellectual Chike Jeffres, this volume brings together essays on the different aspects of philosophy written originally in African languages including Amharic, Dholuo, Gĩkũyũ, Wolof, Yorùbá and Akan. As far as I know these essays are among the very first in modern times that have African philosophers philosophizing directly in an African language. The volume does also carry English translations; but it is worth noting that this reverses the old order— that is, translations from the European into the African language.

I cannot overstress the work on African languages pioneered by John Mugane at Harvard as well in institutions like SOAS, University of London and the University of Cairo. I was surprised at a conference on African studies held in Ghana to meet with the delegation from Egypt, who said that writing dissertations on Africa in African languages is normal at their institution. I hope there develops more contacts between institutes of higher learning in and outside Africa that take African languages seriously as legitimate sources and mediators of knowledge.

But the real breakthrough in the *Jalada* project is not just the fact of translation—this has always been done—it is their emphasis on inter-African-language translations. This centrality, from one African language to other African languages, is crucial if we are going to change the terms of debate and even the paradigm. In this one issue of the magazine, more than thirty African languages were in direct conversation, the most in Africa's literary history. But there were also translations into languages outside Africa—English, French, Portuguese and some of the Indian languages. In short, the *Jalada* translation issue, in a practical sense, has made the arguments that many of us—from Dhlomo and Vilakazi in the South Africa of the 1940s to Cheikh Anta Diop in the 1950s to my 1986 publication *Decolonising the Mind*—have done. And it is simple: that African languages have been and still are legitimate sources of knowledge; that thought can originate in any African language and spread to other African languages and to all the other languages of the world.

But for African languages to occupy their rightful place in Africa and the world, there have to be positive government policies with the political will and financial muscle behind the policies. Publishers and writers too. Academic institutions as well. It has to be an alliance, including patriotic private capital. And I am glad to see that amidst us is Baila Ly from Guinea Conakry, who, I am told, is a very successful businessman and supports African languages. It was a Kenyan business enterprise that came up with an endowment that helped in the founding of the Mabati-Cornell Kiswahili Prize for African Literature.[4] So the entire

4 Now called 'The Safal-Cornell Kiswahili Prize for African Literature'; for more, see https://kiswahiliprize.cornell.edu/; last accessed: 14 June 2022.

language enterprise calls for a grand alliance of government, private capital—particularly Africa based—academies, universities, publishers, writers, translators, interpreters and readers.

A meaningful and practical policy has to start with the assumption that every language has a right to be, and each community has a right to their own language, or the language of their culture. That means equitable resources for their development as means of knowledge and culture. Such languages will not see other languages as threats to their own being. As in border communities, a language of communication across regions can emerge without threatening the individuality of the other languages. In such a situation, it can only strengthen the linguistic network.

You could have, at the very least, a three-language policy for every child: their mother tongue; the lingua franca; and whatever is the most useful language of global reach, that is, the reach beyond their communities. In the case of East Africa, for instance, this would mean mother tongue plus Kiswahili plus English. But there could be other innovations around such a policy: for instance, the requirement of a fourth, which must be other than the mother tongue, that is, any one of the other several people's languages. In any African country we can offer rewards for showing additional knowledge of African languages; we could even link promotion to such knowledge. If you have two equally qualified judges fighting for promotion, then the one who demonstrates competence in African languages within the nation gets extra points. This could be extended to the entire civil service and the academic establishment. And certainly, nobody in the world should get a job as an expert of things African without their demonstrating a knowledge of one or more African languages spoken within their field of research and expertise. Every interview for such academic positions, in Africa and the rest of the world, should include questions like: How many African languages can you read and write? Have you ever published a paper in an African language in the field of your expertise? A combination of some of these tactics and requirements can only result in the empowerment of African languages.

This can help in the complex give-and-take among languages and cultures. Cultures of humans should reflect that of nature, where variety and difference are a source of richness in colour and nutritional value. Nature thrives on cross-fertilization and the general circle of life. So does the human culture, and it is not an accident that cultures of innovation throve at the crossroads of travel and exchange. Marketplaces of ideas were always the centres of knowledge and innovations. In his book *Discourse on Colonialism,* Aimé Césaire once said that culture contact was the oxygen of civilization.

Translation, the universal language of languages, can really help in that generation of oxygen. Translation involves one distinct unit understanding signals from another distinct unit in terms of itself, for instance, within or between biological cells. So, translation is inherent in all systems of communication: natural, social and even mechanical. Nature is multilingual in a multicultural sense but also interconnected through continuous translation. Translation is an integral part of the everyday in nature and society and has been central to all cultures; but we may not always notice it.

But while it is true that translation is the common language of languages, hierarchies of power and domination distort its full function as our common heritage. In more equitable relations of wealth, power and values, translation can play a crucial and ultimate role of enabling mutuality of being and becoming even within a plurality of languages.

In Mũkoma wa Ngũgĩ's article, he also said that 'in translation, there are no indigenous, vernacular, native, local, ethnic and tribal languages producing vernacular, native, local, ethnic and tribal literatures, while English and French produce world and global literature. There are only languages and literatures.'[5]

I will end where I began: securing African languages should be part of a whole vision of Africans securing our resources, for as I told the *Jalada* group when I gave them my story *Ituĩka rĩa Mũrũngarũ*:

> The cruel genius of colonialism was to turn normality into abnormality and then make the colonized accept the abnormality as the real norm [. . .]. The moment we lost our languages was also the moment we lost our bodies, our gold, diamonds, copper, coffee, tea. The moment we accepted (or made to accept) that we could not do things with our languages was the moment we accepted that we could not make things with our vast resources.

5 Mũkoma wa Ngũgĩ, 'A Revolution in Many Tongues'.

So our language policies and actions should empower Africa by making Africans own their resources from languages, making dreams with our languages, to other natural resources—making things with them, consuming some, exchanging some. Then, and only then, can Africa become truly visible in the world in its own terms and from the security of its own base.

Ngũgĩ wa Thiong'o

A Bibliography

Weep Not Child. London: Heinemann, 1964.

The River Between. London: Heinemann, 1965.

A Grain of Wheat. London: Heinemann, 1967.

and Ngũgĩ wa Mĩriĩ. *Ngaahika ndeenda: ithaako ria ngerekano*. Nairobi: Heinemann Educational Books, 1980.

Caitani Mũtharabainĩ. Nairobi: Heinemann Educational Publishers (East Africa) Ltd, 1980.

Detained: A Writer's Prison Diary. Nairobi: EAP, 1981.

and Ngũgĩ wa Mĩriĩ. *I Will Marry When I Want*. London: Heinemann, 1982.

Devil on the Cross. London: Heinemann, 1982.

Decolonising the Mind. Portsmouth, NH: Heinemann, 1986.

'English: A Language for the World?' *The Yale Journal of Criticism* 4 (1) (1990): 283–93.

Penpoints, Gunpoints and Dreams: Towards a Critical Theory of the Arts and the State in Africa. Oxford: Clarendon Press, 1998.

Mũrogi wa Kagogo. Nairobi: East African Educational Publishers, 2005.

Wizard of the Crow. London: Harvill Secker, 2006.

Something Torn and New: An African Renaissance. New York: BasicCivitas Books, 2009.

Dreams in a Time of War: A Childhood Memoir. London: Vintage Books, 2011.

Globalectics: Theory and the Politics of Knowing. New York: Columbia University Press, 2012.

In the House of the Interpreter: A Memoir. New York: Anchor Books, 2015.

'Mũgũnda ũrĩa ũngĩ' [The Other Garden]. *Hawai'i Review* 79 (*Call & Response*) (2014): 10–45. Available online: https://bit.ly/3wreEX2 (last accessed 14 June 2022).

Secure the Base: Making Africa Visible in the World. London: Seagull Books, 2016.

'Ituĩka Rĩa Mũrũngarũ: Kana Kĩrĩa Gĩtũmaga Andũ Mathiĩ Marũngiĩ'. *Jalada,* 22 March 2016. Available at: https://bit.ly/3JXvWAI (last accessed: 6 April 2022).

Den upprätta revolutionen. Stockholm: Modernista, 2017.

Wrestling with the Devil: A Prison Memoir. New York: The New Press, 2018.

The Upright Revolution: Or, Why Humans Walk Upright (Sunandini Banerjee ill.). London: Seagull Books, 2019.

Works Cited

CASTILLO, Otto René. 'Intelectuales Apoliticos / Apolitical Intellectuals' (Margaret Randall trans.). *Berkeley Journal of Sociology* 20 (1975–76): 8–11.

CÉSAIRE, Aimé. *Discourse on Colonialism* (Joan Pinkham trans.). New York: Monthly Review Press, 2000.

DORFMAN, Ariel. 'Last Will and Testament / Testamento' in *In Case of Fire in a Foreign Land: New and Collected Poems from Two Languages* (Edith Grossman trans.). Durham, NC: Duke University Press, 2002.

EVANGELIOU, Christos C. *The Hellenic Philosophy: Between Europe, Asia and Africa*. Binghamton: Institute for Global Cultural Studies, Binghamton University, 1997.

FLECHA, Victor Jacinto. 'It's No Use' (Nick Calstor trans.) in *Radical Arts Group Programme of Revolutionary Poetry*. Zaria, Nigeria: Ahmadu Bello University, 1983.

FLOOD, Alison. 'Short Story by Ngũgĩ wa Thiong'o Translated into over 30 Languages in One Publication'. *Guardian,* 29 March 2016. Available at: https://bit.ly/3DMmjmT (last accessed on 13 June 2022).

GILLIATT, Penelope. 'Nigeria Hits the London Stage'. *Observer,* 19 September 1965. Available at: https://bit.ly/3pv1xjO (last accessed on 13 June 2022).

GRAGAU, Maulline. 'Morocco's Controversial New Education Law Sparks Outrage'. *The African Exponent,* 23 July 2019.

HICKEL, Jason. 'Aid in Reverse: How Poor Countries Develop Rich Countries'. *Guardian,* 14 January 2017. Available at: https://bit.ly/3frE5T3 (last accessed on 20 June 2022).

JACOBS, Sarah. 'Just Nine of the World's Richest Men Have More Combined Wealth than the Poorest 4 Billion People', *Independent,* 17 January 2018. Available at: https://bit.ly/3Dn7oOH (last accessed on 20 June 2022).

JEFFERS, Chike (ed.). *Listening to Ourselves: A Multilingual Anthology of African Philosophy.* Albany: State University of New York Press, 2013.

JOYCE, James. 'Ireland at the Bar' ['L'Irlanda alla sbarra'] (Conor Deane trans.) in *Occasional, Critical and Political Writing* (Kevin Barry ed.). Oxford: Oxford University Press, 2000. Available at: https://bit.ly/3AA5Y3c (last accessed on 14 June 2022).

KENYATTA, Jomo. *Facing Mount Kenya.* London: Mercury Books, 1961[1938].

LYNCH, William. *The Willie Lynch Letter: The Making of a Slave.* Bensenville: Lushena Books, 1999.

MACAULAY, Thomas Babington. 'Minute Upon Indian Education', 2 February 1835. Available at: https://bit.ly/3DMbBN8 (last accessed on 20 September 2022).

MANUEL, Don Jon. '¿Padre hijo o caballo?' ['Father, Son or Horse?'] in Angel Flores (ed.), *First Spanish Reader: A Beginner's Dual-Language Book.* New York: Dover Publications, 1988, pp. 2–5.

MARX, Karl, and Friedrich Engels. 'Idealism and Materialism' in 'Feuerbach: Opposition of the Materialist and Idealist Outlooks' in *The German Ideology*. Moscow: Progress Publishers, 1968. Available at: https://bit.ly/3CgDQDz (last accessed on 13 June 2022).

NGŨGĨ, Mũkoma wa. *Nairobi Heat*. New York: Melville House, 2011.

——. 'A Revolution in Many Tongues'. *Africa Is a Country*, 4 August 2016. Available at: https://bit.ly/3FvZUvi (last accessed on 13 June 2022).

PRATT, Richard H. 'The Advantages of Mingling Indians with Whites' [Text of speech delivered at an 1892 convention] in *Americanizing the American Indians: Writings by the 'Friends of the Indian' 1880–1900*. Cambridge, MA: Harvard University Press, 1973, pp. 260–71.

PRICE, Angharad. *The Life of Rebecca Jones*. London: MacLehose Press, 2014.

SPENSER, Edmund. *A Vewe of the Presente State of Ireland*. Manuscript, 1596; first printed edition, Dublin: James Ware, Society of Stationers, 1633.

WAGNER, Peter, and Wanda Bertram. 'What Percent of the U.S. Is Incarcerated? (And Other Ways to Measure Mass Incarceration)'. *Prison Policy Initiative*, 16 January 2020. Available at: https://bit.ly/3WgkZ2U (last accessed on 20 June 2022).

WENDT, Albert. *From Manoa to a Ponsonby Garden*. Auckland: Auckland University Press, 2012.

ZONDEK, Verónica. 'Fuego' in *Ojo de agua: Antología*. Santiago: Lumen, 2019.

——. *Cold Fire* (Katherine Silver trans.). Storrs, CT: World Poetry Books, 2022.